About the Author: J.J. Brown

J.J. Brown (dates unknown) was a chemist and a man of science, celebrated for his insightful and forward-thinking contributions to metaphysical discourse in the late 19th and early 20th centuries. Based in Govanhill, Glasgow, Scotland, with his postal address at 300 Cathcart Road, Brown blended his scientific expertise with a deep philosophical curiosity, producing works that sought to bridge the realms of science and spirituality.

His book, *The Eternal News*, first published in 1889 and later republished in Scotland around 1911, reflects his commitment to exploring the "great problems of the universe" through rigorous reasoning. The work earned notable recognition, including a commendation from Dr. Alfred Russel Wallace, co-discoverer of the theory of evolution by natural selection, who described *The Eternal News* as "one of the cleverest and briefest metaphysical treatises I have met with... clear and logical."

J.J. Brown's influence extended well beyond his lifetime. His book, *The Eternal News*, was notably mentioned in the preface of Wallace D. Wattles' *The Science of Getting Rich* (1910), a seminal text in the New Thought movement. Wattles' work later inspired Rhonda Byrne's best-selling book and film *The Secret* (2006), bringing Brown's ideas indirectly into the mainstream consciousness of modern metaphysical thought.

Brown was also a contributor to *The Glasgow Weekly Herald* between 1905 and 1910, sharing his thoughts with a wider audience. In his public exchanges, Brown eagerly cited figures such as Sir William Crookes and the Gifford Lectures on Natural Theology, reflecting his engagement with contemporary scientific and philosophical dialogues. These references highlight his commitment to investigating what he described as the "One Sole Substance," a concept foundational to his metaphysical inquiries.

J.J. Brown's unique voice and intellectual rigor situate him among the thinkers who sought to reconcile the empirical observations of science with the profound questions of existence, making *The Eternal News* a timeless work of speculative thought.

The Eternal News - J. J. Brown

Designed and Published by Fauun,
PO Box 678, Mermaid Beach,
Queensland 4218 Australia

Email: fauun.writer@gmail.com

A republication of the original edition
published in 1889, Glasgow, Scotland.

Copyright © Fauun, 2024

This edtion first published by Fauun in Australia 2024

ISBN 978-1-7638101-0-5

Typeset in Cormorant Garamond.

The Eternal News

CONCERNING TIME, SPACE, SUBSTANCE, MOTION AND SHAPES, THE ENTIRE TOTAL OF ALL BEING OR EXISTENCE.

J. J. Brown

PUBLISHER'S NOTE

This edition of *The Eternal News* marks the first time J.J. Brown's profound work has been published since its original release in the late 19th century. The journey to bring this remarkable text back into the world has been nothing short of extraordinary.

By 2024, only two known copies of *The Eternal News* were documented globally: one held in a private collection and the other safeguarded within the National Library of Scotland in Edinburgh. To ensure the preservation and accessibility of Brown's visionary ideas, I embarked on an odyssey of over 16,000 kilometers from Australia to Scotland to view and photograph the rare surviving copy.

As predicted by J.J. Brown himself, I am honored to present to you the *twenty-first-century* edition of *The Eternal News*. This edition is faithful to the original manuscript. You will notice some overtly religious language, often gendered to 'He/Him,' which reflects the cultural context of the time in which it was written. The text has been carefully retyped from photographs, and you may find certain words, language, and punctuation to be archaic or challenging to understand. It did not seem appropriate for me to modernize these elements more than absolutely necessary.

Short of contacting the original author through a séance, I had to make creative decisions on his behalf. Every effort has been made to retain the integrity of Brown's original vision while allowing contemporary readers to engage with his work as authentically as possible.

It is with great honor and reverence for J.J. Brown's legacy that I present this new edition of *The Eternal News*. May it inspire and provoke thought in a new generation, as it surely did in the readers of its time.

— *Bel Bare, Australia. November, 2024*

THE ETERNAL NEWS

CONCERNING TIME, SPACE, SUBSTANCE, MOTION AND SHAPES, THE ENTIRE TOTAL OF ALL BEING OR EXISTENCE.

By J. J. BROWN

Twentieth Century Edition

FOR JANUARY 1, 1901.
(LOOK OUT FOR THE NEXT IN THE YEAR 2001.)

Century by Century

BEING ACTUALLY IS!

OUTSIDE TIME, SPACE, SUBSTANCE, MOTION AND SHAPES NOUGHT IS!

TIME, SPACE AND SUBSTANCE ALWAYS ARE!

SUBSTANCE IS CONSCIOUS SPIRIT!!!

SUBSTANCE BY WILL-ACTION CREATES FORCE AND MOTION!

THE VARIOUS FORMS IN NATURE, SUCH AS STARS, CLOUDS, HILLS, STONES, WOOD & ATOMS ARE BUT MERE SHAPES INTO WHICH SUBSTANCE THROWS ITSELF!

MOTIONS AND SHAPES MAY BEGIN TO BE AND MAY CEASE TO BE:

AND THEY ARE WHAT IS CALLED THE CREATION!

Time and Space, Substance, Motion and Shapes.

Please,

Would whoever undertakes the reading of this book kindly oblige me by going thoughtfully over the TRUTHS set forth therein apart from the COMMENTS thereon, and by simply marking off those assented to as well as those dissented from, and by letting me know the result? It is well for each one to know assuredly what he believes. Opinions sent me will be prized and preserved as likenesses of fellow spirits. Time and Space and Substance and Motions and Shapes will certainly occupy our attention through all eternity.

– J. J. BROWN.

TIME

TRUTH I

TIME IS NEITHER SPACE NOR SUBSTANCE NOR MOTION NOR SHAPES, BUT SIMPLY TIME.

SELF-EVIDENCE OF TRUTH I

Can you think of Time as being Space or Substance or Motion or mere Shapes? No. Time has no comparison to aught but itself, and cannot be defined in terms of aught but itself: and therefore, Time is simply Time.

COMMENTS ON TRUTH I

1. And so in the first place, Time is neither of the other ultimate facts but simply Time. Thus we show what it is by showing what it is not. It stands in its own lonely grandeur known only by comparison with the others.

2. Do you say that Time is not an entity? If so, what then do you mean by an entity?

If you think that an entity is a something that exists as Substance exists, then Time is not an entity in that sense, for Time is not a Substance, but it is a reality nevertheless.

3. Do you think Time resembles Motion? Well, but nevertheless it is not Motion: for Time would still elapse at its own irresistible rate although the universe were motionless.

4. Let us have no misunderstanding about the word "Time". It is not employed here to denote any particular measure of Time such as that of the probation of mankind upon the earth which

is generally termed Time as distinguished from Eternity; but the word "Time" is employed here in its philosophic sense to denote Time itself whether finite or infinite.

5. Moments, minutes, hours, days, weeks, months, years, centuries, etc. Eras historic or geologic, etc. Ages of planets, of suns, of sun systems, etc. Aeons of ages, etc. These are all merely measures of Time. And such phrases as "From everlasting to everlasting", "From eternity to eternity," express the entirety of Time.

6. Time past and Time future are always equal. And are there not just as many centuries in Time as moments? For, of either is there not an infinite number? Are not both equal in quantity then?

7. There is an infinitesimality of Time. A moment may be divided into a million parts, the parts again the same and so on. Ephemeral insects may imagine their short life a long one. Youth fancies the years to be longer than age does.

8. Time is not merely an idea, for Time would be whether we took note of it or not. Time is Time: Duration is just another name for the same reality.

9. Do you say that the infinite is unthinkable? It is quite thinkable, though not fathomable.

10. Let us say that the Future is a "single infinity," because it hath beginning at the Present but no end; and let us say that the Past is also a "single infinity," because it hath end at the Present but no beginning; and let us say that Time as a whole is a "double infinity," because it is beginningless and endless: and so we shall be learning our first lesson in the Science of the Infinities.

TRUTH II

TIME IS ENDLESS

SELF-EVIDENCE OF TRUTH II

Can you think of Time as having an end? No. Why, try to suppose Time having an end and you will perceive that any supposed end will mark a point from which, think as you like, there would still be Time beyond or after. So therefore, Time is endless: as it is unthinkable otherwise.

COMMENTS ON TRUTH II

1. Ever! Ever and Ever! Forever! Forever and Ever! Forever and Forever! Evermore! Forevermore!

2. The Infinite is quite thinkable by us, but not fathomable by us; for were it fathomable, it would not be Infinite. We can think of Future Eternity, and know that it has no end; but we cannot fathom it or find the end of it, so to speak. We know that the Infinite is. And that it could have an end is quite unthinkable.

3. It is a truth unalterably sure that there is an eternity to come, and whether we reflect upon it or not, our conscious essence will nevertheless be in some form or forms during that eternity.

4. By the way, a word upon the practical using of the Present. Yet what is the actual Present which stands between the Future and the Past? Has it any magnitude of length? However, take the present hour or third part of an hour and concentrate attention upon the duty to be done in that hour or third part of an hour and get it done, then immediately decide on the duty to be done in the next hour or third part of an hour and get it done as before, and so on. This is how to make Past, Present and Future Sublime.

TRUTH III

TIME IS BEGINNINGLESS

SELF-EVIDENCE OF TRUTH III

Can you think of Time as having a beginning? No. Why, try to suppose Time having a beginning and you will perceive that any supposed beginning will mark a point from which, think as you like, there would still be Time before. So therefore, Time is beginningless: as it is unthinkable otherwise.

COMMENTS ON TRUTH III

1. Do you say that you do not understand it, that you cannot grasp it? Well now then, if so, let us see what it is that you are trying to understand, that you are trying to grasp. In thought you go away back, and back, and back along the Past. Why, do you not perceive that you are trying to understand it as having a beginning, that you are actually trying to grasp a beginning, while all along you clearly understand that it has no beginning, and all along you firmly grasp the fact that it could not even have a beginning?

2. That Time could have a beginning is what is quite unthinkable, and not that Time has no beginning which is fact. Must it not be one or other of these ways?

3. You who are saying that you cannot understand how there could be any Time at all before the creation began to be, is it not the case that you are looking upon Time as if it were simply the duration of the Created World? Time is even something more than the mere duration of a thing although it be that. However, look upon Time as being duration of Space, and then see if you

can think of a Time when there was no Space, and perceive that as Space must always have been so must Time.

4. Hear what White says :-

"The Eternal God had no beginning
He hath no end. Time hath been with Him
For everlasting; like Him 'twas uncreate;
Like Him it knew no source;
What is it then? The Past eternity
We comprehend a Future without end:
We feel it possible that even yon sun
May roll forever: but, we shrink amazed —
We stand aghast when we reflect that Time
Knew no commencement: that heap age on age
And million upon million without end,
And we shall never span the void of days
That were, and are not but in retrospect.
The Past is an unfathomable gulf
Beyond the span of thought! 'tis an elapse
Which hath no mensuration but hath been
forever and forever."

5. Apprehend or comprehend the Infinite? Why, we know that the Infinite is, which is as much as to say that we know that it is Infinite.

6. Some one yet is punning over the term "Time," and swearing that Time begins at birth and ends at death, and that it is Eternity which lies behind these. Such an one is right too in a way; but very far wrong in failing to notice that in philosophy the term "Time" is applied to duration in Eternity as well. However, such as one no doubt believes that Eternity then is beginningless and endless, and so we won't quarrel over words.

SPACE

TRUTH IV

SPACE IS NEITHER TIME NOR SUBSTANCE NOR MOTION NOR SHAPES, BUT SIMPLY SPACE.

SELF-EVIDENCE OF TRUTH IV

Can you think of Space as being Time or Substance or Motion or mere Shapes? No. Space has no comparison to aught but itself, and cannot be defined in terms of aught but itself: and therefore, Space is simply space.

COMMENTS ON TRUTH IV

1. Space is simply Space! Do you ask ironically if it could be anything simpler? Well, suppose we should say that Space is Room, or that Space is Expanse, or that Space is Capacity, would we not just be giving other names to the same reality? And might these not be objectionable names? And would it not be just a little more confusing and bewildering than the simple statement that Space is simply Space?

Suppose then we say that Space is the Place where Substance is: will that do? Substance is! Why, of course you are asking now about the Space where no Substance is! All right: we perceive that you know very well what empty Space is, and what filled Space is, or on the whole, what Space is.

2. Need we supply you with lines, areas and volumes to show up respectively the three dimensions of Space? Very well, take Length there, now take Length and Breadth and Depth and Height likewise, and you will get the three dimensions. Whoever tells us there is a fourth dimension should also tell us where and how to find it.

TRUTH V

SPACE MUST ALWAYS HAVE BEEN, AND MUST ALWAYS BE.

SELF-EVIDENCE OF TRUTH V

Can you think of Space as ever having not been, or as ever becoming to be not? No. Why, try to suppose space as ever having not been, or as ever becoming to be not, and you will perceive that Space could never not have been, and that it can never not be. So therefore, Space must always have been and must always be: as it is unthinkable otherwise.

COMMENTS ON TRUTH V

1. That Space could ever not exist is quite unthinkable: For were there no Space, would there not still be Space?

2. Eternal Space! Uncreated Space! Calm, Immovable Space! Everlastingly the Home of God.

TRUTH VI

SPACE HAS NO BOUNDS.

SELF-EVIDENCE OF TRUTH VI

Can you think of Space as having bounds? No. Why, try to suppose an end or bound to Space in any direction whatever, and you will perceive that nothing could be a barrier to Space, and that any supposed end or bound would but mark a place from which, think as you like, there would still be Space beyond. So therefore, Space has no bounds: as it is unthinkable otherwise.

COMMENTS ON TRUTH VI

1. That Space could have bounds is quite unthinkable. Any solid barrier would by itself in Space, and no Space at all is unthinkable. On and on, outwards and outwards and outwards, never an end, Space, boundless, illimitable, infinite. The fact is appalling.

2. There are six principal directions in Space relatively to one's self. Direction Upwards, direction Downwards, direction Forwards, direction Backwards, direction Right, and direction Left: these are the six. But betwixt these directions, why, there is an infinite number of other directions all stretching out from one's self in straight lines. Here are ever so many "single infinities," if you like to call them, as they have at one's self a beginning, but from thence they go on to infinity. Here, too, if you like, are ever so many "double infinities" by considering such directions as joined to their opposite directions making beginningless and endless lines.

However let us take Space as a whole; and instead of the "double infinities" crossing each other at one's self, let us think of them as stretching side by side, parallel for ever, and we shall perceive what an infinite quantity of them Space is able to hold within its limitless sides. How appalling is Space! Let us look on it as a sphere expanding and widening with circle ever outside circle, outwards towards the Infinitely Great, and as contracting and narrowing with circle ever inside circle, inwards towards the Infinitely Great, and as contracting and narrowing with circle ever inside circle, inwards towards Infinitely Little. But every atomic volume is an inlet to an Infinitely Little, and what an infinity of infinite-simalities must there then be in Space! Space altogether is an unutterable infinity of infinities.

3. There is more than room enough in all Space then for endless extensions of filled space along with endless extensions of empty space. And would not an endless extension of filled space contain an infinite quantity of Substance, however much it

were limited in its width? Nought but the Entire All of things is in a sense "absolutely infinite," or nought is in a sense "absolutely infinite" but that which includes All that is. Whether there be endless extensions of filled space along with endless extensions of empty space, or whether the one be limited in extent, thus leaving the other infinitely infinite, we shall never be able to know of ourselves. Considering Substance as consisting of solid particles there must be vacuities along with it or Motion would be impossible. So there is empty space and there is filled space. And considering the infinitely small as of endless extent in its way, there will certainly be an infinity in this way of empty space and of filled space.

4. We ourselves, our own conscious beings, possess, occupy, fill portions of Space. Here is a curious fact we may note in passing. If we with eyes shut will think of distant points in the directions Forwards, Backwards, Right, Left, Upwards and Downwards, strongly and quickly we shall feel ourselves, our conscious beings, moving within our heads, turning towards these directions. Or, if we strongly think of some object of our sight, and then of some object of our hearing, and do so alternately for a little, we shall feel ourselves, our conscious beings, passing backwards and forwards twixt the optic and auditory nerves. Or, if we fly off in fancy, or recall some old memory, we shall feel ourselves, our conscious beings, our souls, our spirits, retiring up into some vague, undefined places somewhere in the cellular roofs of our brains. This fact we heard and tried it and found it so.

5. However, it was Space not Spirit we were speaking upon (yet mark, Spirit is a something which occupies Space). We cannot think of Space having bounds, therefore, Space has no bounds as is quite thinkable, though not fathomable, for were it fathomable it would have bounds. We can think of empty space and we can think of filled space. But what makes filled space? Why, a Substance only makes filled space. Whatever occupies a space, whatever makes filled space must be a Substance.

TIME AND SPACE

TRUTH VII

TIME AND SPACE EXIST OF NECESSITY.

SELF-EVIDENCE OF TRUTH VII

Can you think of Time and Space as existing not? No. Why, try to suppose there being no Time and no Space, and you will perceive that in the place, so to speak, of each respectively there must still be Time, there must still be Space. So therefore, Time and Space exist of necessity: as it is unthinkable otherwise.

COMMENTS ON TRUTH VII

1. The existence of Time and Space, although marvellous, is not at all mysterious.

The problem of their existence is very plain. Why should Time and Space be? Simply because they couldn't not be. And because they couldn't not be, therefore, they must be.

2. Time and Space are; Time and Space exist. They belong to Being or Existence therefore. Who says Substance only is Being or Existence? We can think of Time and Space apart from Substance altogether. Motion, however, though neither Substance nor Space, cannot be thought of apart from Substance and Space.

3. Time and Space are self-existent so to speak. They are not powerful beings or gods because of this. Power refers to action or Motion and belongeth to Something Solid. Time and Space are neither capable of thought nor of action. They are merely Time and Space. Yet it was actually seriously discussed once whether Space was or was not God.

4. We do not attempt to believe that the Great Something that necessitates Time and Space for its existence is the Creator or Cause of Time and Space. For nothing inside Time and Space could create Time and Space; and there is nothing outside could do so, for there is no outside of Time and Space at all. That there could ever be no Time and no Space is quite unthinkable. Utter nonentity in that sense is utterly unthinkable.

TRUTH VIII

ALL BEING, OR EXISTENCE, IS INSIDE TIME AND SPACE.

SELF-EVIDENCE OF TRUTH VIII

Can you think of any Being, or Existence, as outside Time and Space? No. Why, try to suppose any Being, or Existence, as outside Time and Space, and you will perceive that, any Being, or Existence, at all must be inside Time and Space, and that, there cannot even be an outside of Time and Space. So therefore, All Being, or Existence, is inside Time and Space: as it is unthinkable otherwise.

COMMENTS ON TRUTH VIII

1. This Truth is so plainly evident that it needs no comment. Comment would seem ludicrous. When could anything be unless it had a Time to be? And where could anything be unless it had Space to be in? Time and Space are the first conditions or necessities of all Being, or Existence. They underlie all else. They are the outer frame of all things. That there could be any Being, or Existence, outside them is quite unthinkable. All Being, or Existence, is inside them; and if you like, Time and Space, are in themselves.

2. Distance is the quantity of intervening Time or Space, and it is a word which frequently lets us feel the reality of Time and Space.

3. The philosophers distinguish for us two sorts, so to speak, of Time which they call Absolute and Relative. We believe that their Absolute sort is the only genuine, and that their Relative sort is stolen from the genuine by a sleight of hand, and therefore by right belongs to the genuine. Absolute Space, they say, is the infinite and immovable Space in itself considered without regard to the position of any material thing; while Relative Space is that which our senses define by the position of material things to one another, which may be moving (?) through Absolute Space by the material bodies still keeping the same relative distances from one another.

Absolute Time, they say, is Time in itself considered without regard to any motion of material bodies, this flows marvellously at one unvarying rate; while Relative Time is that which our senses define by motion of material bodies.

4. "Time flows marvellously by at one unvarying rate." Here is an excerpt upon that: — "The flux of Time cannot be accelerated nor retarded. Let us suppose the heavens and the stars to have remained without motion from the very creation: does it hence follow, that the course of time would have been at a stand? Or rather, would not the duration of that quiescent state have been equal to the very time now elapsed?"

SUBSTANCE

TRUTH IX

SUBSTANCE IS NEITHER TIME NOR SPACE NOR MOTION NOR SHAPES, BUT SIMPLY SUBSTANCE.

SELF-EVIDENCE OF TRUTH IX

Can you think of Substance as being Time or Space or Motion or mere Shapes? No. Substance has no comparison to aught but itself, and cannot be defined in terms of aught but itself, and therefore, Substance is simply Substance.

COMMENTS ON TRUTH IX

1. Of course, as Time, Space, Motion, and Shapes are not Substance, only Substance is Substance.

Do you say that Substance is a Thing proper? You may have that definition if you choose, yet, Time, Space, Motion, Shapes are still Realities though. Is it the "Something Solid?" Well, yes; it is. Substance is a "Solid Something" which moves. It is the main and central object. Time and Space on the one hand, Motion and Shapes on the other, but Substance central and principal.

2. Substance otherwise "Matter." "Matter" must have weight, must cohere or hold together. But think not that what is called "Matter" must have weight, must cohere or hold together. If you so think then call not Substance Matter, for Substance is the "Something Solid" whether it have weight, whether it cohere, or hold, or press together firmly or not. Let it be jammed into a corner where it cannot escape, and see if it is not a something impenetrable, "solid."

3. Weight and coherency, which in whatever way they are looked upon are but modes of Pressure, require a cause. Pressure requires a cause. And Substance, otherwise Matter, may be made to have weight or coherency, or any other mode of Pressure, simply "at will."

4. What about the Substance of Spirit, so to speak? Is not Spirit a something which moves? But must its Substance have weight or coherency? Well it may have if it itself, that is, the Spirit Substance, chooses to hold itself tight together, or to move itself and push or press against anything.

5. Now then, are you beginning to think that there is not only just Substance, but that there are Substances? Nay, there is only just the One Substance underlying all your Supposed Various Substances. Do you suppose that wood, stone, iron, water, etc., are different Substances? Nay, wood, stone, iron, water, etc., are but different complexities of infinitesimal Shapes, and the Substance that underlies their complex infinitesimal Shapes is essentially the same in each. The apparent difference lies alone in the minute texture or small shapings which compose each, and the manner in which the same is held together. Put it this way, Various infinitesimal Shapes conglomerate together and make apparent different Substances, but underlying each single one of the infinitesimal Shapes is One Essential Substance.

6. "Substance" alias "Matter": either of these two terms we will apply to that "Thing" which "exists" in Space, and to which some apply the title of "Being" or "Existence" solely, and which others consider as the only "entity" extant. Certainly, there is just the one "Substantial" Existence or Entity extant; but space "exists" too, and though not a Substantial Existence, it is still an "Existence." Substance or Matter let us define as "that" which existent in Space has the property of impenetrability, and which manifests Force or Motion at Will.

7. And at once let us get rid of the notion that it is inert. Certainly it is passive, but it is active too. We are active beings yet we are carried passively round the sun; and all of us could be flung hither and thither like passive masses at any time. Matter or substance inert? Why, its gravitating together shows its life everywhere. It is cohering. It is all alive. It is holding itself tight together in every atom; in every

star. And yet they have said that Matter or Substance is inert — What do they mean?

TRUTH X

SUBSTANCE CAN NEITHER COME OUT OF NOTHING NOR GO INTO NOTHING, THEREFORE MUST ALWAYS HAVE BEEN AND MUST ALWAYS BE.

SELF-EVIDENCE OF TRUTH X

Can you think of substance as coming into being out of nothing, or as going out of being into nothing? No. Why, try to suppose Substance as coming into being out of nothing or as going out of being into nothing, and you will perceive, simply, that it could not, any more than that a thing could be and yet not be at one and the same time. So, therefore, Substance can neither come out of nothing nor go into nothing, and therefore, must always have been and must always be: as it is unthinkable otherwise.

COMMENTS ON TRUTH X

1. Substance can not go out of being into nothing: for, how can it? It may be altered into an infinite variety of Shapes; it may be drifted hither and thither in Space and intermingled with itself enormously: but, there is no getting rid of it; it remains always.

The first foundation fact of Chemical Science is that "Matter is indestructible."

Without this, say the chemists, chemistry as a science could not exist. It has been satisfactorily proved, Roscoe I think says, that an annihilation of matter never occurs, and that in the burning of anything and in other chemical actions the materials simply pass into a state in which they are invisible to our eyes but their presence may be ascertained by other means.

2. Substance cannot come into being out of nothing: for, how can it? Where would it come from? If it came from anywhere, it must have been there before. It need scarcely be stated that it is almost wholly from the atmospheric air that the vegetable kingdom is increased in its growth, there being diffused in the air over each acre of the earth's surface a quantity of some 20,000 lbs. of carbon atoms which are the material with which the vegetable world is chiefly composed. *Nihil ex Nihilo*—Nothing from Nothing. Do you say that God could bring Substance into being out of nothing?

What then about His own Substance—the Substance of the Great Spirit, God?

Did it come into being out of nothing? Did He Himself—Did His own Spirit-Substance emerge out of nothing? "No," you say, "He is eternal, His Spirit-Essence is eternal."

Very well, then, His Spirit-Substance is eternal: think upon this and you will perceive that He out of his own Substance might shape a universe, and out of His own Substance might give parts to be other Spirits.

3. That Substance could come into being out of nothing or go out of being into nothing is quite unthinkable. And as therefore Substance does exist, it must always have been and it must always be.

4. Now, to Theism and Non-Theism alike let me say that a thing cannot be and yet not be at one and the same time, and that two and two cannot be more than four nor less than four, but must be but four of absolute necessity, and that likewise Nothing can be created out of Nothing of absolute necessity. Or when anyone shuts their eyes to the light because they would rather not see what they cannot help seeing, why, what then? That does not alter the facts before them. They will stumble over them in the dark all the same and bruise themself in some way or other most assuredly, if they do not even meet in with fatal disaster which I scarcely see how they can long escape if they do not open their eyes.

5. In our youthful reasonings about Being or Existence we come very soon to perceive that Time and Space are eternal and self-existent so to speak, and that therefore they required no Creator or God. Then when we come to reason about Matter, about the Material of the universe, if true to our convictions, we conclude it to be eternal and self-existent likewise, and that therefore it does not require to have had Creator or God either. And if we just stop here upon the surface and go not any deeper into the subject we become Atheists, materialistic Atheists.

Truly in this case "A little learning is a dangerous thing." but "Drink deep or touch not," does the poet sing? Yes—and as we begin to drink deep it occurs to us that Matter may be conscious, drinking deeper we perceive that the assertion that "matter is Conscious" cannot be disproved, and that though Time and Space are co-eternal with Matter, yet, Time and Space are not things conscious, are not things which have Power or Motion, but that Matter or Substance must have Power, must have Will-Force or it could not move itself into Shapes as it does.

TRUTH XI

SUBSTANCE OCCUPIES OR FILLS WITH ITSELF ITS OWN SPACE.

SELF-EVIDENCE OF TRUTH XI

Can you think of Substance as otherwise than a something that occupies or fills with itself its own space? No. Why, try to suppose Substance not occupying or filling with itself its own space, and you will perceive that it could not thus have being or existence at all. So therefore, Substance occupies or fills with itself its own space: as it is unthinkable otherwise.

1. In fact, if you want a definition of Substance, if you think that the name itself, "Substance", is not a sufficient definition, or this either, "Substance, that which can move". Then here you are, surely this is sufficient, — Substance is that which occupies or fills with itself the space that it does occupy or fill. For, that how Substance could exist without occupying a space is quite unthinkable. So do you see now that Substance is the something solid which neither Time nor Space nor Motion no Shapes are.

2. In natural philosophy the physicists have it as their first, great property of matter that a mass thereof at one and the same time cannot occupy the same identical space that another mass occupies, or that two bodies cannot occupy the same place at the same time, and this they term the property of "Impenetrability." Truly, this is the first and principal property thereof, if it can be called a property at all, for it is neither more nor less than stating the essential existence of Substance, its indestructibility and uncreatability.

3. If you like, this "Impenetrability" of Substance can be demonstrated by jamming into a corner solid, liquid, gaseous, or "etherial" forms of Substance; although it will be difficult to

get a corner in which to jam the Ether as all glasses, metals, etc., are too porous for it.

TRUTH XII

SUBSTANCE DOES NOT FILL ALL SPACE, OR IT COULD NOT BE CAPABLE OF MOTION.

SELF-EVIDENCE OF TRUTH XII

Can you think how substance could be capable of Motion if it filled all Space? No. Why, try to suppose how if Substance entirely filled or occupied the whole of space it could be capable of Motion, and you will perceive that, without there being empty space the Substance would be altogether blocked, that, any portion of the Substance being incompressible and surrounded at every point by Substance incompressible could never move out of its place at all unless there were empty space. So therefore, Substance does not fill all Space or it could not be capable of motion: as it is unthinkable otherwise.

COMMENTS ON TRUTH XII

1. Whenever Motion takes place must it not be by a definite mass of Substance however small that moving mass may be? And though the moving mass gets split up infinitesimally, are not the infinitesimal parts definite sized though small? Yes. And since Motion thus always necessitates definite sized masses for the moving, so the definite sized masses necessitate vacuum or vacuities for their free play.

Let us suppose any large, cubical space, such as an ordinary sized room, to be filled entirely full of small cubical blocks of solid wood all of an equal size, how then, the room being exactly filled, could any of the small cubical blocks of solid wood move or shift their places unless there were vacuum equal at least to the size of one of them? Were they but the size of chemical atoms, still, if one would move, there would require to be a vacuum equal at least to the size of one of them. So we take it that if definite sized masses would Move, though their substance be not firm and coherent like wood or atoms, it would be found the same in this respect.

2. Let us put it this way absolutely. If Matter were absolutely continuous with Space, if there were no absolute vacuities or vacuum, it is absolutely correct that there could be no Motion, and that the Material Universe would be absolutely fixed. For, the whole being impenetrable or solid, it would be absolutely incompressible. And how could one part of impenetrable, incompressible Matter, surrounded on all sides by terrible, impenetrable, incompressible Matter, Move out of its place, out of this terrible, altogether, absolute solidity-immovableness, unless it or the surrounding Matter became temporarily penetrable or compressible; and if Matter thus became temporarily penetrable or compressible there would then temporarily be an absolute vacuum of absolute necessity.

3. Fluidity is produced by giving substance free scope with Empty Space. In chemistry the particles of a solid body separating a certain degree apart make a liquid body, and separating further apart they make a gaseous body. This would be impossible were there no room for the particles to separate apart. The fluidity of finite spirit does not necessitate subdivision. Finite spirits with free scope in which to move may elongate themselves like a spider's thread, or surrounding vacuities within them may ramify like a sponge, and thus mingling freely with empty space appear perfectly mobile and continuous. Substance, as it is impenetrable, is incompressible;

And is on that account akin to Solidity itself. Apparent compressibility is on account of vacuities therein; but were Substance compressible without vacuities within it, that would be equal to its annihilation which is unthinkable. And so if the whole of Space were entirely filled with such a solidity of impenetrable Substance it would be altogether one huge block up. Neither eddies nor circulatory motions of any kind could be within it, for supposing that there could, then, the edges of those rubbing against their environment of Substance and being continuous therewith would set the whole environment a-moving, which would be the whole universe a-moving, which would be impossible, substance filling all Space.

4. For Fluidity and Action then there requireth free scope with Empty Space. Portions in the interior of a mass of Substance must remain immovable unless there be vacuities therein, or unless they be released by the sides of the mass yielding into Empty Space. And any mass of Substance may freely Move in all its parts if any portion of its surface bound upon any Empty Space. That how Substance could move were there not some unoccupied Spaces, is quite unthinkable.

TRUTH XIII

SUBSTANCE, THOUGH IT FILL NOT ALL SPACE, MAY HAVE NEVERTHELESS AN ENDLESS EXTENSION THROUGHOUT SPACE.

SELF-EVIDENCE OF TRUTH XIII

Can you think how Substance, though it fill not all Space, may have nevertheless an endless extension throughout space? Yes. Why, try and suppose it, and you will perceive that a shaft of Substance of any limited width might begin and have an extension onwards forever in one of the unending directions of Space, or a Shaft of Substance of any limited width might come from the endless depth of one of the unending directions of Space and have an extension onwards forever in an opposite or other direction of space; and, of either or of both such shafts of Substance there might be a finite or an infinite number existent in space. So therefore, Substance, though it fill not all Space, may have nevertheless and endless extension throughout Space: as is quite thinkable.

COMMENTS ON TRUTH XIII

1. With this truth we are well able to conceive the perfect possibility of there being an Infinite Substantial Being apart from, and therefore not inclusive of, other substantial beings. Or, from this truth it appears that an infinite substantial being, such as God, to be infinite does not necessitate the absolute occupation of entire Space to the exclusion or inclusion of other substantial beings. Space is able to hold an infinity of infinities. A shaft of Substance of infinite length though finite in thickness is nevertheless of infinite quantity; and being infinite in quantity though limited at the sides it nevertheless bears the title of, and is Infinite. And say, being thus infinite in quantity can the detaching of finite portions therefrom ever make it less than infinite?

How many links would require to be taken from an endless chain to destroy the endlessness of the chain? All spirits out of The Great Spirit and The Great Spirit infinite still!

2. Strange to say, there could even be shafts of Substance each thus of infinite quantity in length, but each of different thicknesses; and having different thicknesses, some would be greater and some lesser than others though everyone of them would be infinite in quantity. Does it not appear plain that an infinite Shaft

of Substance of a certain degree of thickness would have double strength of power in overcoming in collision another infinite shaft of Substance of only half that certain degree of thickness?

3. Who knows what immense substantial beings there may be in Space? Who knows but that there may be an infinite quantity of immense substantial beings in Space? Who knows what stupendous politics may be the rage all over Space? At any rate is there not a tremendous antagonism going on betwixt our God and Satan? But, our God—the God who upholds the world for us in which we dwell as well as the other worlds; and who upholds these bodies of ours through which we are enabled to behold and come into harmony with His creation; the God in whom we live, move and have our being: this our God deserves our loyalty. Are there more Gods than one? Well, at any rate, this much we believe from the testimony of our very eye-sight, that our God, the God in whom we live, move and have our being is ONE in and through all the range of stars to as far as the waves of light extend. For, that Force of gravity or cohesion, the product of Spirit-Power, One Force holding or binding all the stars in their range and the etherial particles, as well as the very substance of each etherial particle so as to make the same elastic that it may vibrate into light.

4. As for the triune nature of God—Certainly, Universal Substance might possibly be divided in Space into Three equal and infinite divisions, so as that there might be Three Great Spirits, and these Three, in equal and infinite power and glory, One. But, to be One in actual person, and at the same time, to be Three in actual persons, cannot be. Is it not more consistent with the necessity of things to consider Father, Son and Spirit as three aspects of the One Great Being? Is it not That Great Being,

Universal Substance, in whom we live, move, and have our being, is One God; and in His Omnipotent Will-Power as working through all nature we could consider Him as Father;

and in His Omniscience working in the hearts of men we could consider Him as the "Spirit", manifestation of Himself, and in His not through a burning bush, but through a human organism, manifesting His wondrous character to men and working out their salvation, we could admire Him, and adore, and could consider him thus as "Son". Still, Christ, if He was a man, was entirely One with God in aim and purpose of Will: *See John xvii. 27-23.*

5. But to return to Truth XIII, its argument stands thus. That how the existence of unoccupied spaces in Space would hinder Substance from still being of endless extent throughout Space is quite unthinkable. Then, there is empty space in which God is not, in which there is nothing but empty space so to speak? Yes. But from Truth XIII, we see that God may be infinite in extent notwithstanding. God's omnipresence and infinity do not necessitate that He be all and everything

Of Being or Existence. Why, if you take omnipresence and infinity in that sense you exclude, you leave no room for the existence of any man, angel or devil. You leave no room for yourself. God does not occupy the actual, absolute, identical space that the you yourself, your own spirit-substance occupies. His Spirit surrounds yours, environs yours. Then again, although there is empty space God can move into and occupy that empty space, of course leaving empty space behind Him. And so He has full command of all Space.

6. An infinite Substance in Space, being conscious and being itself infinite in extent, will comprehend and fathom Infinity in a way that a finite substance never can, and will be able, perhaps, to know the necessity why there should be Substance inside Space and Time. And so "A God alone can comprehend a God." A finite substance though stretching out into infinitesimal thinness like a spider's thread, and though it should never break,

but continue always to stretch out into the infinite, it could never become an endless, infinite thread.

7. If this great Substance in Space be a thing conscious, if it be Spirit, it should be able to move of itself, and this it does. It moves itself into Shapes and Holds itself in Shapes. This fact will be felt further on. But, were it moved thus by a thing external to itself, by a spirit external to itself; then this thing, this spirit, moving, must be a Substance.

TRUTH XIV

WHETHER SUBSTANCE HAVE OR HAVE NOT AN ENDLESS EXTENSION THROUGHOUT SPACE WE CAN NEVER BE ABLE TO KNOW OF OURSELVES.

SELF-EVIDENCE OF TRUTH XIV

Can you think how we can ever be able to know of ourselves whether Substance have or have not an endless extension throughout Space? Why, try to suppose how we ever can; and you will perceive that though we travelled at the greatest possible speed forever and ever and ever to explore the unending directions of Space we could never be able to know any more than we now do whether Substance have or have not an endless extension throughout Space, because we would never be able to reach all the unending endlessness of Space to know whether Substance have or have not an endless extension there. So therefore, whether Substance have or have not an endless extension throughout Space we can never be able to know of ourselves: as it is unthinkable otherwise.

COMMENTS ON TRUTH XIV

1. That conscious entity of one's self, that substantial thing beneath the skull-dome and somewhere within the brain, that thing which thinks, (and it must be a substantial thing for anything unsubstantial could not think?), that something, that substance which is one's conscious self is exceedingly apt and able at feeling conscious of the differences of various things with which it deals. In fact, to be conscious of the differences of things which come into contact with the conscious self is nothing more or less than Thought. Between certainty and conjecture there is a broad difference which strikes a conscious being plainly. That space is without bounds is a certainty which is felt from feeling the very nature of Space as it were, but that Substance is of endless extent in Space or that it is limited in its extent in Space is felt to be a conjecture from feeling the very nature of Substance, though from feeling that it is in Space it is no conjecture that it must be one or other of these ways. And so with all our considerations of Being or Existence we easily feel what is certainty and what is conjecture.

2. No finite being however immense is able of itself to know whether Substance be infinite in extent in Space or not. If the Great One tells us He is so, we will believe Him knowing His character, but in a strict sense "belief" is not "knowledge".

Conscious beings are conscious of course at every point of their being; but what an awful consciousness must an infinite being have who is conscious at once all over the endless extent of his being! Such a being will be able to grasp, feel and fathom the infinite in a way that a finite one never can. I am speaking here literally of the largeness or infinity of actual bulk of individual, personal substance, for conscious being must be essence or substance of some sort: if you like, call it spirit-substance.

Man's Spirit is a part off or from God's Spirit. Man is therefore able in a way to comprehend like God. Yet, considering God as infinite in very extent, Man in another way is not able to comprehend like God.

3. However, how we ever can know whether Substance actually be or be not of endless extent throughout Space, is quite unthinkable. This Truth gives us to know the nature of the " unknowable" so to speak. Here is the "unknowable" — How Substance may be arranged all over Space. And yet, here, it is only the actual mode which is unknowable; the various possibilities which may possibly be are knowable. Therefore there cannot be anything existent in the " unknowable" which is unthinkable. The infinite is quite unthinkable by us to be infinite; we know that it is infinite. But it is not fathomable by us because it is unfathomable. Were it fathomable by a finite it would not be infinite.

4. Under this Truth XIV, let me say that fancy and imagination are very fine, but reality alone can satisfy. We will not concern ourselves at present with the curiosities, or conjectures of the unknowable. To speculate on what variety of starry Shapes there may probably be towards the infinite ends of Space, or to speculate on what variety of events may happen in the so remote future which is as yet even beyond the range of God's own determinations, may be in its own place. But we will deal at present only with fixed, absolute certainty. Every one of us is bound to deal with the realities and certainties of Being or Existence. For if we refuse to deal with them, they at any rate will most assuredly deal with us in actual experience. For, we ourselves actually exist. We Positively Exist!!!

5. Let us now pass from The Infinitely Great to the Infinitely Little.

TRUTH XV

YET, EVEN THE SMALLEST PARTICLE OF SUBSTANCE IS OF AN ENDLESS EXTENT IN ITS WAY, FOR IT GOES TO THE ENDLESS DEPTH OF THE INFINITESIMAL.

SELF-EVIDENCE OF TRUTH XV

Can you think how even the smallest particle of Substance is of an endless extent in its way, or how it goes to the endless depth of the infinitesimal? Yes. Why, try to suppose the smallest particle of Substance, and at any rate you will perceive that it must have length, breadth, and thickness, and might therefore be divided, each of its divisions must still have length, breadth and thickness, and so each of them might therefore be divided, and each of their divisions divided the same again, and so on forever; as it is unthinkable a particle becoming so small as to lose length, breadth and thickness, or to lose its very being, which very being is the possibility of its further division. So therefore, even the smallest particle of Substance is of an endless extent in its way, for it goes to the endless depth of the infinitesimal: as is quite thinkable.

COMMENTS ON TRUTH XV

1. "Even the smallest particle" —Critic, note here the verbiage; can there possibly be the smallest? For, that there is a limit to the depth of the infinitely little is quite unthinkable.

2. There is no end here. A full realisation of this is seldom or ever grasped, and yet its full realisation is absolutely necessary to the comprehension of the apparent complexity of Substance. Beyond the range of the telescope there is an infinite space, so also beyond the range of the microscope there is an infinite space.

And immense as is the field of view that the microscope opens up, it is but a finite portion of the infinite beyond.

3. In the dim distance are the chemical molecules and atoms: and we are about as far from seeing them with our naked eyes as we should be of the words and letters of a newspaper placed about a third of a mile distant. In gases and liquids the chemical atoms and molecules though close together nevertheless do not touch but roll and move about like little worlds actually kept in their appointed orbits by a kind of gravitation. And in solids the chemical atoms and molecules though they may be said to touch, as they hold firm to each other, they do so only at certain points of their surfaces, so that there are numerous interspaces large or small according to the sizes of the atoms or molecules, and the interspaces form pores in the solid, regular or irregular according to the shapes of the atoms or molecules as also according to the way in which they have come together or solidified.

4. Now, the Undulatory theory of Light which obtains amongst the moderns necessitates the supposition that the chemical atoms and molecules float in a fluid called the Luminiferous Ether, wavelets or vibrations in which produce Light; and that this Ether thus circulates freely through the pores of solids, and lashes wavelike around all atoms and molecules and fills the vast spaces betwixt planets, suns and systems, that it is a great fluid in which all the stars and atoms are immersed, and which, in the revolution of the earth round the sun or in the revolution of worlds round worlds, passes through the interspaces of the atoms composing the earth or the worlds as freely as air passes through the trees of forests. How terrifically minute must the Ether particles be? Perhaps immensely as far beyond the chemical atoms in the awful depth of the infinitesimal as the chemical atoms are beyond our naked eyesight. Even an Ether particle is infinitely divisible conceivably. It is elastic and so has parts which hold together. There is no such thing conceivable as a final,

indivisible point. And there never can be such a thing. There is no end here.

5. Take a few actual, practical illustrations to the Truth. Gold may be hammered so thin as that the fifty millionth part of a grain may be still visible. Two grains of a spider's thread would reach from London to Edinburgh. A grain of carmine red can be divided by solution of water into four million visible parts. A single grain of musk will scent the air of a room for years without losing any appreciable quantity of its weight and fresh air being continuously admitted. And by spectrum analysis we can prove the presence of the two hundred millionth part of a grain of certain metals. Why, a million live animalcula do not exceed the bulk of a grain of sand, and has not each animalculum a body and soul? Someone has shown that in a mass of animalcula no bigger than a grain of sand there may be ten thousand times more blood corpuscles than grains of sand in the mountain of Teneriffe.

6. There is no end here. There is no ultimate atom or particle. Every atom or particle however small is a mass of Substance; and were our spirits small in proportion, each atom or particle might seem a mountain; and no doubt there will be minute spirits to whom the chemical atoms will actually be worlds.

The chemical atoms actually worlds? Yes. And those atom-worlds made up of prodigiously smaller atom-worlds again, and these others the same, and so on to infinity. And now, with that idea do you think we could sound the depth of the infinitesimal? No. There is no end.

7. Some who have gazed upon the infinitely little have turned from it exclaiming that "Matter or Substance consists just of so many ultimate points of Force." Such is not the case; there is no such thing (and can be no such thing) as an ultimate point: for however small a point may be there might still be a smaller. So a child might exclaim after gazing upon the starry universe that "It consists just of so many points of light." By the way, would

those who start their theory of the universe on the assumption of a multitudinous number of various ultimate atoms or points of force all tending to aggregate peculiarly, explain what causes their tendency to peculiar aggregation, and more especially, what causes the Substance of which each of their ultimate atoms or points consists to hold or cohere so rigid together so as to form such ultimate atoms or points?

8. But here is an important fact which flows from Truth XV. The smallest speck of Spirit-substance is in itself of infinite depth. The smallest animalculum of Spirit-essence, so to speak, has in itself an infinity of parts. And so the smallest spirit will be infinite in its infinitesimally and will be able thus to claim citizenship with the infinities. The smallest speck of spirit-substance being infinitesimally infinite will have room sufficient within itself for hoarding if it likes an interminable record of experiences. Perhaps this is why the human spirit is able to wrestle with infinitude.

9. Substance or Matter then occupies a space, but does not occupy all Space. It may be of endless extent throughout Space nevertheless. But whether it actually be of endless extent throughout Space or not we never can know. Still it goes to the endless depth of the infinitely little. Proceed to the next Truth now.

TRUTH XVI

SPIRIT IS SUBSTANCE, BECAUSE IT MUST OCCUPY OR FILL A SPACE.

SELF-EVIDENCE OF TRUTH XVI

Can you think of Spirit as otherwise than a something which must occupy or fill a space? No. Why, try to suppose that it does not occupy or fill a space, and you will perceive that it can not then have being or existence at all. So therefore, Spirit is Substance, because it must occupy or fill a space: as it is unthinkable otherwise.

COMMENTS ON TRUTH XVI

1. Spirit, or that which is conscious, or that which is capable of being conscious of the differences of various things when they affect it, which consciousness of the differences of things we call Thought: that then which thinks, viz., Spirit, must be in Space, as there is nowhere out of Space.

Spirit, being a something inside Space, and not being Space itself nor Time, nor mere Motion, nor a mere abstract Shape, though it have Shape, or rather, though it can throw itself into any Shape it chooses: being a something which actually exists inside Space it must occupy or fill the space that it does occupy or fill, and therefore has the property of im-penetrability, and so must be a Substance of some sort.

2. Yet wrangling materialistic and spiritualistic moderns; what about Spirit-Substance? What about the Substance of Spirit? What is the nature of the Substance of Spirit or Spirit-Substance, for unsubstantial or immaterial Spirit is nothing at all? Conscious Sprit must be something substantial, and therefore material. Matter is Spirit: is it not? what is Matter? Or what is Spirit?

3. Each Spirit, being a mass of conscious Substance, must have length, breadth and thickness, and must therefore have a Shape; but the Shape will be continually changing according to the voluntary, the spontaneous movements of the Spirit. And a Spirit, being a continuous mass of conscious Substance, will be conscious at every point of itself: so that any point or part of

its surface being touched or acted upon, the whole mass will be conscious of the touch.

4. Each Spirit, being thus through and through a tremulous mass of conscious Substance having the power of voluntarily moving itself or parts of itself, and of thus throwing itself into any Shape it chooses, being thus one conscious mass, will in the exercise of its voluntary power of moving itself and of altering its Shape, as well as in the contacts it comes into with other Substance, be subject to sensations of variable degrees—pleasurable or painful.

Now, the opposing or thwarting of its "will" when it attempts moving itself or any part of itself will, no doubt, give to the conscious Spirit-substance sensation painful to the degree in which it is thwarted and opposed: and the aiding or abetting of its "will" when it attempts moving itself or any part of itself will, no doubt, give to the conscious Spirit-substance sensation pleasurable to the degree in which it is aided and abetted. That is the whole mystery of pleasure and pain.

Then, the first and chief lesson which the individual mass, so to speak, will learn by its experience will be that of keeping its whole Substance intact, of holding it firm, of (so far as it is able) never allowing any part to get severed and become totally detached, for, it will find that the greater its mass, so the greater its scope and its power.

And so, while altering its Shape, while elongating itself, or pressing itself through pores, or finding itself in collision with other Substance, or being in a surge of other Substance, its constant care will be to hold and have all its own Substance attached or intact. As it has the power of spontaneous movement, as it is able at will to move itself or any parts of itself, it will therefore be able to hold all itself together if it chooses, except some other Substance interpose and prevent. And while being thus continually intent in holding all its Substance together, while its will in this respect has become a fixed, habitual law throughout its being, then any external thing attempting to divide it or server a part will, no doubt, be sorely against the "will," and accordingly will give pain to such and such a degree.

But what if some parts should be divided therefrom? Well, what else can the severed parts become but separate individuals, holding their own Substance and acting for themselves by experience in every respect the same as the mass of which they are the same Spirit-substance—essentially the same, only that they are smaller and have thus less scope and power.

Witness the division and sub-division of some of the lower forms of the Protozoa, the Amoebae for instance, for an almost literal illustration of the case. Almost? Yes.

For the only difference is that the spirits of the Amoebae are entangled with protoplasm, which is of other substance than that of their spirits, as our bodies are of other substance than that of our spirits.

5. Spirit, being thus through and through a tremulous mass of conscious Substance having the power of voluntarily moving itself or parts of itself, and of thus throwing itself into any Shape it chooses, will, it is evident, be able to make its Substance rigid or pliant at pleasure, part rigid and part pliant; or any amount of parts within itself it will be able to make rigid or pliant. Supposing now a Vast Spirit (and Spirit must be Substance) having made itself thus rigid and solid in some parts of its Substance, and having allowed itself to be passive and pliant in other parts of its Substance, and supposing we ourselves were living and moving and having our being in amidst the Substance of such a Spirit, would we not while getting upon the rigid portions thereof consider the same to be solid ground, and would we not see in the solid ground according to its size and contour hills, mountains and valleys, as the case might be?

And as for the pliant portions thereof, would we not find amongst them liquid, gaseous and etherial and other fluids as the case might be? So much for that: yet, Is it not suggestive of what actually is?

6. Our own and other spirits inhabiting organised floating tenements are too actively engaged attending to and adjusting their tenements to the various other environments as to come to the practical feeling of the actual Substance of their own Spirit-selves. But were they removed out of their tenements and taken for a time into pure empty space, so as that their conscious selves could not be engaged with any external, environing Substance at all; then each one would very soon arrive at the self-consciousness of its own Substance. Would each one see itself? Well, there would be no luminiferous ether to vibrate light for that purpose; but each one would feel and know itself in a manner which we all may yet after death experimentally try for ourselves.

7. Yet another idea. What Shape or Shapes should Spirit-Substance be most apt to throw itself into, seeing that it has inherent within it the prevailing purpose to hold all its Substance together to prevent any getting detached, and seeing that there is the external surge of other Spirit-Substances surrounding it liable to damage it, and more so if it be found in a disadvantageous Shape? Well, do you not think, that, with this prevailing purpose to hold together pervading all parts of its being, all parts of its being therefore will hold and press and crouch in together, and by so doing will form a perfect sphere, a globule? And the centre of which globule will be what but a centre of gravity, so to speak, towards which all parts of the Spirit-Substance will press in or weigh in heavily?

8. To go deep into the whole subject we perceive that what constitutes "Individuality" is the "Will". The "individual wills" prevent actual contact of spirits with spirits from becoming actual connection. A Spirit, however small it may be, is

nevertheless a mass which as a whole has its own "will". And so this is it which keeps the various spirits while they move in constant contact with each other from coming into actual connection with each other. Betwixt "contact" and "connection' there is a vast difference and individuality of wills in this respect makes the same apparent.

9. The human spirit being lodged within the brain must therefore continuously roll or graze against its environing walls, yet it is not conscious of any great pain on that account. The shivering of the optic nerve against the spirit gives it the sensation of light, and the shivering of the auditory nerve gives the sensation of sound. And such like sensations are pleasurable when not carried to extreme. And such like sensations are caused within the spirit, by the spirit being affected with motions from without. Now the question comes, how will we, in our reckless freedom revelling in amidst the spirit-substance of the Great One— How will we affect Him? He must be conscious thereof. Yes, but as He is so infinite in comparison to us, all our motions taking all together may affect Him only like wavelets of a summer's breeze.

Still, by doing or not doing what He wills us to do, we can verily give Him pleasure or pain. Methinks that if a mass of the Universal Substance as large and as firm as the earth were violently riven asunder against the Will, that that would cause Him pain.

10. When we reflect upon the immensity of the Mind of the Universal Being we are dazed. All the geologic stratas of the innumerable worlds with all their records must be within His consciousness, and all the memories stored in every organism are also before Him as His memory.

What a Mind is this!

TRUTH XVII

SUBSTANCE IS SPIRIT, BECAUSE IT MOVES ITSELF INTO SHAPES.

SELF-EVIDENCE OF TRUTH XVII

Can you think of Substance starting to Move of itself without it being conscious? Why, try and suppose Substance isolated in empty space and there starting to Move of itself, and you will perceive that if it starts to Move of itself, being isolated in empty space, it must do so out of its conscious Will. So therefore, Substance is Spirit, because it Moves itself into Shapes: as it is unthinkable otherwise.

COMMENTS ON TRUTH XVII

1. "The universe consists of a Substance in movement" said a French philosopher. But the question is, What is the cause of its Movement? or How did it start into Motion?

No doubt, we can conceive the possibility of Substance as one whole mass moving on in a straight line through an infinite empty space from everlasting to everlasting; Eternal Motion is only possible thus. And the material universe as it now is, may or may not be moving as a whole in this way. Yet though it actually were so moving, what good would such Motion do? As for an Eternal Motion of Substance in one whole around its own axis, there is the question, What would keep the Substance a-holding together? That question answered would show Motion's origin. And yet, were there even an Eternal, axial Motion of Substance, what good would such Motion do? But, the movement or Motion we would account for is that of Substance amid Substance. Within itself in Space the Universal Substance is actually now in movement. And therein Motions opposing Motions prevent

Motions. And had this whole Motion been from everlasting, surely by opposing itself and preventing itself thus, it had destroyed itself or reached equilibrium long ago. The question is, What started or What stirs up this Motion? Why, what else could but a Will-Power? Will-Power actually exists: and what is an Act at Will but an origination of Motion?

2. But besides all this, what about The Holding Together? Not only is it evident that the universal Substance is moving for a Purpose, but it has already Moved itself into various Shapes in which it is firmly holding itself. Here is the question of questions:

What makes the Substance hold together in a shape or shapes? That is the question of questions. What makes the substance in the atom hold or cohere or gravitate so firmly together that the atom seems almost impossible to be broken. And what makes the atoms hold or cohere or gravitate together into variously Shaped little masses, called molecules, which make all the apparent differences of Substance?

And what makes these molecules hold or cohere or gravitate together into larger masses? And what makes the larger masses hold or cohere or gravitate together into worlds? And what makes worlds hold or cohere or gravitate together into systems? Surely no one thinks that the universal Motions getting tired take to Resting themselves for a time in this fashion by crushing Substance together. What causes this gravitating, cohering, or holding together of Substance? Why, what else could but a Will Power? At "Will" a conscious agent is able to act or press so as to start Motion, and is also able to continue the pressure though the Motion is resisted. And so, "Will" is the cause of the holding or cohering or gravitating together of Substance: I defy any conscious being to think or conceive or produce any other cause capable. And as we have already seen and will yet further see that Spirit must be a Substance which can make itself rigid or pliable at will: so then, this universal Substance or Matter in Space must be a Spirit-Substance as it has moved itself into Shapes of sublime order, and as it holds itself so together as naught else but conscious Spirit-Substance could do.

3. But might there not be two actual occupiers in Space a conscious Substance and an unconscious Substance? And might it not be the former which moves the latter into Shapes and holds it in Shapes? Such questioning is a frequent stage in the progress of thought, upon which many have sat down. When we look upon the universe and behold that tendency of universal Substance to aggregate together, we may first, as it were, suppose it to be a necessary law of Substance so to do; then at length we perceive that an adequate cause is necessary; and so we conceive a pervading Spirit as that cause.

So far so good: but sitting down here we will shrink spirit into an immaterial nothing. Spirit is that which acts, acting it must Move; moving it must be a moving Thing, a Substance. And it is the universal Substance itself which acts, moves, and holds together in Shapes.

4. Now, does anyone suppose "This Holding Together" to be caused entirely by surrounding pressures? If so: how now will an atom revolve with the idea? However, it is just the surrounding pressures we would wish to have explained. What is the cause of them? Eternal Force of Motion does some one say? Why, when the Force of Motion opposes the Force of Motion, the Force is destroyed. But "Will" originates "Force". Do you not acknowledge that? Then do not obstinately, deliberately and falsely deny. Eternal Motion could never create Will-Force. And note well, Conscious Spirit actually does exist; it actually exists.

5. With some this "Holding, Cohering, or Gravitating Together" of Substance is especially termed "Force". This "Force" cannot be aught but the continuous action of Divine Volition. It is this "Force" which gives the firmness to matter and so makes it elastic. The result of a Will-action of Spirit is a pressure, a "Force"

which would cause Motion if not resisted. The Acting or Action of Spirit is what? Shall we call it "Will," or shall we call it "Force"? It is Will-Force. It is the Creator of the Energy of Motion. But the Energy of Motion others will also term "Force": and so here is where the confusion is.

6. The Identity of Matter with Spirit: this is the gist of it all. Matter is actually conscious: this is what we are driving at. Here it is—Substance, actually Spirit; its coherency being Will-pressure: the earth and the heavens but a mere system of Shapes caused thereby. Why, Spirit moves and acts and nothing can move and act but a Substance.

Modern science resolves the universe into Matter, Force and Motion. This in other words is simply Spirit-substance, Will-pressure and Motion.

7. Substance can attenuate itself then infinitesimally and through infinitesimal so pass pores of Substance, and at Will throw itself into rigid visible Shape again.

Think even of the luminiferous ether circulating through interatomic spaces and perceive how a spirit could come in, the doors being shut, and then throw itself into any Shape. The very fact of "Motion" is proof the substance has Will-Force, or that Substance is Spirit. Substance can and does Move itself into Shapes. "Matter is Mindstuff" says one. Matter is Spirit then, because it Moves itself into Shapes. Here we come in sight of Motion and Shapes, the two last departments of Being or Existence: Time, Space and Substance being the first three. By the way, the Sphere appears to be the most frequent Shape chosen. The purpose may be because that that Shape is less liable than any other to be dis-shaped by accident; or because the Sphere is of all Shapes the Shape of beauty and order; or because of necessity flowing from the action of the Substance holding itself all together. At any rate the fact of the Sphere-Shape prominent throughout nature is in itself proof of Mindstuff being builder and architect. "Nature centres into balls" says Emerson; and if I remember aright these also are his words which follow—" could we but know the meaning thereof?"

8. Substance is Spirit: yes, it is the "that" which thinks, the that which is conscious; and it can only be conscious of things which affect it, thing which come into contact with it. That Substance or Matter is Spirit cannot be disproved. Whereas it is evident that Substance or Matter has all the properties usually ascribed to "immaterial" (?) Spirit; that it Moves itself of its own accord or has voluntary motion; that it can assume any shape it chooses; that it can hold itself firmly together in Shapes, or that it is alive with cohesive or gravitative force; and that the various Shapes into which it has actually thrown itself are the visible objects which make up what we call the Creation. This is the climax and copestone of science, this is the finish and fulness of philosophy—downright, absolute Truth.

9. Spirit is Matter, and this is the gist of it all. The popular creed which holds Spirit to be a something immaterial is wrong at the very basis. And the basis being wrong, the whole superstructure upon it, if not wrong also, must nevertheless be in a dangerous condition. ever much the meaning of the term "immaterial" may be construed, the popular notion takes it to be "wanting impenetrability." But with the right notion of what Spirit is, there is the foundation for a strong, unshakeable religion.

10. As for "caused or uncaused volition", it is against commonsense and experience to suppose that we have no choice in our actions. We think that we are free, and we cannot think otherwise. The reason or motive for action the spirit itself chooses, and therefore in that sense creates its motive of action. The spirit itself is a free agent in its own acts. If circumstances drive it against its choice and overpower even the opposition of its will-action it is not there responsible. But in the multitude of things in which it has choice there it is responsible. Of various,

equal uneasiness or motives weighing upon the spirit, the one which moves it to action has been created heaviest by the spirit itself. The spirit itself gives the casting vote to one or other of the reasons which affect it and thus goes off in action, and this it does of its free choice.

TRUTH XVIII

SPIRIT IS NEITHER TIME NOR SPACE NOR MOTION NOR SHAPES, BUT MUST BE SUBSTANCE.

SELF-EVIDENCE OF TRUTH XVIII

Can you think of either Time or Space or Motion or Shapes or aught else except Substance, as being conscious Spirit? No. Why, try to suppose Spirit as being either Time or Space or Motion or Shapes or aught else except Substance, and you will perceive that Spirit must be a Substance. So therefore, Spirit is neither Time nor Space nor Motion nor Shapes, but must be a Substance: as it is unthinkable otherwise.

COMMENTS ON TRUTH XVIII

Can you think of Time as being a conscious something? No. Can you think of Space as being a conscious something? No. Can you think of Motion as being a conscious something? No. Can you think of a mere abstract Shape as being ca conscious something? No. But you think of Substance as being in itself a conscious something? Yes.

Again, can you think of Spirit as being but Time? No. Can you think of Spirit as being but Space? No. Can you think of Spirit as being but Motion? No. Can you think of Spirit as being but a mere abstract Shape? No. But can you think of Spirit as being a Substance? Yes. It must be a Substance.

It is ridiculous to think that Time thinks, or that Space thinks, or that Motion thinks, or that mere abstract Shapes think, but not quite so ridiculous to think that Substance thinks. In fact, it is utterly ridiculous to think that aught else but a tangible something can be capable of thinking or of being conscious.

But how does Substance think? This cannot be explained in terms of Motion any more than it can ever be explained in terms of Motion how Spirit thinks. It is enough to know that Substance is Spirit, is the thinker, is the actual conscious thing itself, and that by being conscious of things which affect it, it thus thinks. The objects of which one is conscious may come and go, but the being conscious of them is not a process of Motion at all.

2. Spirit is—What? It is that something which is conscious. Think on this again: it is the thing which is conscious. But, conscious of what? Conscious of external objects which affect it. Why, it must be a Substance. Substance is Spirit, that is, Substance is conscious. But consciousness (note the word) does not necessarily signify self-consciousness, for there can be consciousness without self-consciousness. It signifies "being conscious " of anything. Some time may be taken to arrive at the consciousness of Self. We can be conscious of a multitude of things before being conscious of Self.

3. What now do you know about Matter? And what now do you know about Spirit?

This much, that the one is the other, or that they are one and the same. Spirit must be an object in existence as Matter is. And Matter is Spirit. Is not this materialism and Spiritualism with a vengeance? This position is unique. Whoever holds it must look out for being jammed betwixt materialists and spiritualists. It is now no more Matter and Spirit, for matter is Spirit. Matter is

Spirit and spirit is matter: much matter lies in the spirit of this truth which to a true spirit matters much.

4. What is Motion? 'Tis but the mere shifting of Substance from one place to another, and however complex Motion may become it can never be aught else but the mere shifting of Substance; and yet some so-called Thinkers are trying to think that Spirit or Conscious Being is the product of complex Motion. Others again are trying to think that Spirit or Conscious Being is the product of some complex Shape or Shapes into which Substance is cast. Upon such flimsy fallacies myriads of minds are being gibbeted. Why, it is just this: spirit or soul exists; it cannot be Time, it cannot be Space, though it must be in these; it cannot be Motion, it cannot be a mere Shape, though it be capable of moving and of taking a shape; it cannot be any mere abstraction of existent Substance: it must therefore be Substance itself. Again, Spirit or Soul must occupy a space; and as it is inconceivable of it being mere Time, or Space, of Motion, or Shapes, its occupying a space shows it has the property of impenetrability, and what has that property we call Substance or Matter, and hence, Substance or Matter is spirit or soul. Spirit or Soul or Mind or Intelligence-which? Well, all more or less apply to that which is conscious. Yet an idea is not a Substance: an idea is the Spirit's consciousness of some reality, but the Spirit is Substance.

5. Being or Existence is — sure as the most certain sure. I am. I know that I am:

I am therefore a conscious being. If I have not always been I must have at any rate been from universal conscious being. And so conscious being must have been and must be eternal, —sure as the most certain sure. This conscious being of one's self is conscious only of what is presented to it, or of what comes in contact with it.

How could it be otherwise? It may also be conscious of impressions left upon it by things which have come in contact with it.

Still, its consciousness is only of things which directly affect it. It is in itself a conscious being; yes, but conscious of what?

Why, of things which affect it. When things affect it, it will be conscious of the comparative differences of the effects they produce upon it, and it will thus be enabled to infer pretty much what the things are in themselves. If left alone in blank, empty space, as that nought substantial will affect it from without, it will of course be unconscious of any tangible environment, as in that condition there will be no tangible environment to be conscious of, but, as it is in itself a conscious something, a Substance, it will certainly come to be conscious of itself and of Space in which it is in, by moving some part of itself against some other part of itself,—sure as the most certain sure. A conscious, existent entity cannot but be conscious of the Ever-present Always or of the Always Ever-present. But give me an environment, and let it be The Great Spirit, God, chiefly.

6. To conclude, Substance or Matter is the that that thinks, the that that is conscious or Spirit. For, that is how Substance can move itself as it does into Shapes of creation, or that is how Substance can cohere, gravitate or hold itself firmly together as it does in those Shapes, except it be Spirit: is quite unthinkable. And, Spirit, or the that which thinks, the that which is conscious is Substance or Matter. For, that how Spirit can exist as it does in Space otherwise than a Substance occupying a Space, or that how Spirit can Move and act as it does, except it be Substance: is quite unthinkable.

TIME, SPACE & SUBSTANCE.

TRUTH XIX

TIME, SPACE AND SUBSTANCE CONSTITUTE UNCREATED BEING OR EXISTENCE.

SELF-EVIDENCE OF TRUTH XIX

Can you think of Time, Space and Substance as constituting created being or existence? No. Why, try to suppose Time, Space and Substance as having been created, and you will perceive that their supposed Creator must have been uncreated and must also be or have been Themself a substance in Space and Time.

So therefore, Space and Substance constitute uncreated being or existence: as it is unthinkable otherwise.

COMMENTS ON TRUTH XIX

1. That an uncreated Creator of any creation could be aught else but a Great Substance in Space and in Time is quite unthinkable.

2. Truth XIX. coupled with Truth XXXII. makes the sublime fact that "Time, Space and Substance" is the Increate, and "Motion and Shapes" the Create. The Everlasting Substance in Space and in Time throws itself into a transitory system of Shapes in Motion; which Shapes in Motion are the earth and the heavens or what we call the Creation. Underlying and making all the transitory Shapes of creation is this Everlasting Substance.

3. Behold, inhabiting Time and Space the Great One whose works are Motion and Shapes! That this Great, Conscious Substance, this Great Spirit does exist, it must always have existed, and always must exist. The Name by which He named

Himself reaches a height of philosophy above which we cannot get. Here it is-listen, "I AM That I AM", or as the revised version has it, "I AM Because I AM". Had this Great Being never been, Motion and Shapes had never been, and what then had been a blank Time and Space but blankness indeed. Oh! This is the Eternal Glory in Time and Space, This Great, Conscious Substance. This is the "That" that "Is".

4. Our spirits and all other spirits must have been parts detached from the Great One, the Great Spirit-Substance, or they must have been of themselves from everlasting. For, could God create from nothing a being greater than Himself? No.

Could He create from nothing a being equal to Himself? No. Did He create Himself at all? No. Could He make Himself greater by creating from nothing more Spirit-Substance to Himself? No. Could He annihilate Himself or even make Himself lesser by annihilating any portion of Himself? No. Well then, neither could He create out of nothing our or other spirits, nor annihilate the Substance of our or other spirits.

So, our spirits and all other spirits must have been parts from the Great, Universal, Spirit-Substance detached, or they must have been of themselves from ever-lasting.

Why, when we consider that His Spirit-essence never was made or created, how do we consider other Spirit-essences to have been made or created? But what if the whole is but a universe of conscious atoms? "Then each atom asserting its indisputable right to dance would form a universe of dust," and so Young in his Night Thoughts concludes that "A Godhead reigns."

5. This mighty Spirit-substance diluted in Space with multitudinous Motions—what then? This Immense Mass and the masses detached—what then? The Infinite may give forth the finite and be the Infinite still. Yes. But finite spirits having emanated might be absorbed again. Would it be justice? Ah! I think we must leave

it to Love. Yet, will there not be numerous portions of the Great Mass attenuating, detaching and connecting again ere self-conscious individuality sets upon them? Do not all the spirits of the animal creation which come forth mailed for a time in various organisms, do they not all merge in Him again?

Says Milton :—

And if our substance be indeed divine

And this etherial essence cannot fail—

What then?

Shelly, did you think that :—

The pure spirit shall flow

Back to the burning fountain whence it came,

A portion of the Eternal which must glow

Through Time and change unquenchably the same?

Then—What then?

6. A human spirit is a definite Mass of spirit-substance, and therefore it is perfectly plain that although the Substance is forever indestructible the Mass is not. The Mass may be divided and sub-divided and scattered abroad and thus destroyed; yet, the particles of spirit-substance wherever they be cannot cease to be bits of conscious being. The individual being of a human spirit then is dependent upon that Great Power that environs it, that Great God in whom it lives, moves and has its being. How long could it hold itself together against His might? A full realisation of this should make us humble and willing to do His will. And, "The gift of God is Eternal Life through Jesus Christ our Lord."

7. From "Natural Law in the Spiritual World" we gather this grand and glorious idea. This piece of conscious entity which constitutes the Me myself, or that piece which constitutes the You yourself when in correspondence with the vibrations of the air by the medium of the ear it is then alive to sound: when in correspondence with the vibrations of the ether by the medium of the eye it is then alive to light: and when in correspondence or communion in intelligent consciousness or spiritually with the Great Spirit by the legal medium of Jesus Christ it is then alive to God. But when broken off correspondence with these, it is dead to sound, dead to light, dead to God; even although it be literally immersed in God. What is the main concern for us then? It is this: to be conscious continually of being in right relationship with God.

This is Eternal Life.

8. What is a conscious being if it have nothing to be conscious of? It is well that we have a great environment of Universal Substance of which to be conscious and in which to delight. While as for the Universal Substance, The Great Being Himself, what can He be more conscious of, and in what can He have more delight, than the beings that live, move and have their being in him. Thou God seest us.

MOTION

TRUTH XX

MOTION IS NEITHER TIME NOR SPACE NOR SUBSTANCE NOR SHAPES, BUT SIMPLY MOTION.

SELF-EVIDENCE OF TRUTH XX

Can you think of Motion as being Time or Space or Substance or mere Shapes? No. Motion has no comparison to aught but itself, and cannot be defined in terms of aught but itself, and therefore, Motion is simply Motion.

COMMENTS ON TRUTH XX

1. Motion. Here now is another great reality. Strictly speaking Motion is not a thing; only Substance is the thing. Motion is nevertheless a grand reality.

2. Substance, Space and Time are absolutely essential to it. It is a possibility flowing from those three. Let us think and we will perceive that without those three Motion would be impossible. There could be no Motion without a Substance to move and a Space to move in and a Time taken for the moving.

3. Also, according as the quantities are altered of Substance, Space and Time which come into combination, so to speak, or which give the conditions necessary for Motion, so there are varieties of Motion. Given a definite mass of Substance shifting over a mile of Space in one minute of Time and we get Motion; but if again but one second of Time be given we still get Motion but a different kind from the former on account of the different

quantity of Time introduced; and were the quantity of Space or of Substance changed we would have other variety likewise.

4. There are glorious possibilities of Motion seldom thought upon. Immense distances may, so to speak, be brought nigh. Masses shift over millions of miles in a moment. Some starry Distance avails not on account of the glorious possibilities of Motion. This department of Being or Existence, this sublime reality, Motion, is extremely marvellous. Atoms can vibrate millions and millions of times in a second.

It becomes a question, when we think of the enormous and terrific possibilities of Motion in its speed, whether or not there can be a limit to its swiftness; as also, when we consider the infinitesimality of Space and Substance, whether or not there can be a limit to its slowness.

5. Motion is proof of the existence of God. "The universe consists of a substance in movement," say the philosophers. Herein is Motion of practical account. Motion is merely the shifting of a mass of Substance from one place to another. And not only can we guide and direct, impel or impede Motion already begun, but we can, if we choose, shift masses of Substance from one place to another, and so we by our wills can create Motion. We ourselves however being small, our will-actions have but small scope. The Great Being over all, and through all, can by His will-action heave worlds millions and millions of miles in a second, and set atoms a vibrating millions and millions of times in a second.

6. Motion is one-half of the creation. Immense is the Motion of systems, suns, planets, etc., in all their variety of revolutions; of oceans, seas, rivers, etc., in all their variety of billowy surge and cataract; and of the wind in all its variety of whirling and sweeping tempest. Yet not less immense is the Motion of the minute, or so called ultimate particles in substate of which we have light in all its variety of Colour, Sound in all its variety of Tome, Heat in all its mild and fierce potency, and Electricity and

Magnetism in all their yet undiscovered wonders. What marvellous phenomena from Motion of the minute, or so-called ultimate particles of Substance! Motion is one-half of the creation, the mere Shapes or configuration of masses and particles being the other half.

7. Now, betwixt Substance and Motion lies this Truth :—

SPIRIT BEING A SUBSTANCE, VARIETIES OF MOTIONS BEATING AGAINST IT GIVE IT VARIETIES OF SENSATIONS.

For, can you think how Spirit being a Substance, varieties of Motions beating against it would otherwise than give it varieties of sensations? No. Why, try to suppose varieties of Motions to be beating upon the surface of a conscious Substance without it being conscious thereof, or without it feeling sensations therefrom, and you will perceive that the Substance being conscious must, of course, then be conscious of the varieties of Motion beating against it, must therefore have the consciousness thereof, or feel effects or sensations therefrom. So therefore, Spirit being a Substance, varieties of Motions beating against it give it varieties of sensations: as it is unthinkable otherwise.

This then must be the result, Substance being Spirit; well; rather, Spirit being a Substance, which it must be. Influences, shall we say, from complex modes of Motion of the minute, or so-called ultimate particles fall upon the conscious-being.

This results from the nature of conscious-being. Motions affect the conscious-being thus. The lightning-flash and the thunder-roll are mere motions, but how they thrill the soul! So, by varieties of Motions from without beating upon the conscious-beings of ourselves, we become conscious of varieties of sensations. And as there is the possibility of there being endless varieties of Motions, there is therefore the possibility for us of endless varieties of sensations. There will then be always something new for us in futurity; for the infinite complexities of Motions which can exist have not as yet come in contact with or affected the conscious Substance of ourselves, and so, of the feelings or sensations which they can effect in us, we, having not yet had experience of them, can have no idea or conception further than that they will be of certain characteristic and peculiar degrees of pleasure and pain. Can we think of limits to the degrees of pleasure or pain any more than to the degrees of the swiftness or slowness of Motion? If there be no limits, then from the very nature of the case we cannot have as yet experienced all sensations possible for us to experience.

Now, that our spirits should be mailed with bodies, it would seem necessary under present conditions. For, were the conscious Substance of ourselves exposed naked to all the haphazard of the environment to which the body is, it would be in a state of utter confusion and danger. The vibrating of air which gives Sound, and the vibrating of the ether which gives Light, would both vibrate against it simultaneously, so that it would not be well able to distinguish betwixt both. But being encased in an organism where by special inlets of eye and ear those respective vibrations are let in to it, filtered, so the speak, by themselves, the spirit has then the possibility of knowing and distinguishing betwixt them. To man on this earth, it would seem that the body is essential to his well-being, as houses or habitation are. But the body is a mere floating tenement, Moved about here and there by its inhabitant spirit. Yet though Moved about thus, there are floods of force and Motion in the body which are not caused by the inhabitant spirit, as there are floods of force and Motion in the fire and steam of a locomotive engine, which are not the direct effect of the engineer who uses and manages them.

TRUTH XXI

MOTION THOUGH BEING IN SPACE FILLS OR OCCUPIES NO SPACE.

SELF-EVIDENCE OF TRUTH XXI.

Can you think of Motion being in Space as filling or occupying any space? No. Why, try to suppose so and you will perceive that if Motion filled or occupied a space it would then be a something the same as Substance, but as it us, it is merely the shifting of Substance from one place in Space to another place in Space. So therefore, Motion though being in Space fills or occupies no space: as it is unthinkable otherwise.

COMMENTS ON TRUTH XXI

Motion then is the mere shifting of Substance from one place to another place. How now ridiculous and false is the idea of some atheistic thinkers who have tried to think "consciousness" to be the actual and created product of some kind of complex Motion; as if Motion, which is a mere shifting, a mere unsubstantiality, as if such could ever produce the substantial fact of consciousness by whatever conceivable complexity into which mere shifting could shift. "Motion produces nothing but Motion," say the philosophers in answer to them. But Motion does not even as much as produce Motion. Motion continues itself on into Motion, but cannot produce Motion, for how can it product itself when it is already produced. Instead of Motion producing "consciousness", it is "consciousness" that produces Motion. And further, consciousness only, consciousness can alone produce Motion.

2. Of course, Motion may be said to produce impressions on the consciousness. Aerial vibrations and etherial vibrations beating against or acting upon the conscious substance through the medium of the ear and eye produce in the conscious substance the sensations of sound and of light; but without the conscious substance which alone has the consciousness, what consciousness could Motion ever produce? In fact, Motion or anything else in being is known to be in being only by the "conscious knowing" of the knowing conscious substance which conscious knowing we call "consciousness".

3. And this, then, the mere shifting of Substance is Motion; and it is produced by the will-power of a something conscious. Well, but if there be no free place for the Substance to shift into, if its passage be altogether blocked and opposed, then although the Substance has received a blow of pressure-force by the action of will, or although the will continues to give a pressure-force against the Substance, nevertheless, there is no Motion and can be none until the Substance actually shifts its place: for instance, a man pressing against a huge stone to overturn it; he may press or push never so hard, there is no Motion of the stone until it shifts or moves.

4. And here now is the great fact of the existence of "Force"; and herein is the difference betwixt it and "Motion". Force proper is the pressure of Substance against Substance, and therefore not actual Motion. If this pressure-force were not opposed it would produce Motion. Hence, it has been agreed that about the best definition of "Force" is "That which produces or resists Motion." But from the fact of Substance being Spirit we find the cause of "Force." Its cause is a "will." It is will-action. This "Pressure" of Substance against Substance, this "Force" increases or decreases, begins or ceases just as "will" chooses to press or give pressure. And, if the pressure-force is to be persistent the "will " requires to continue the energy: for instance, I clench either of my hands,

or I clasp them both together firm; the pressure thus produced is caused by my will, and it begins or ceases, increases or decreases just as my will chooses, or rather, just as I choose, or as I "will " to do so, or still more correct, just as "I do" so. Now, if I determine to continue a certain uniform degree of pressure in thus pressing my hands together, and the while that my will-action is so doing, some other individual interposes and with a greater degree of "force" pushes open my hands or holds back my fingers, they will nevertheless weigh or press against the power which thus interposes, and the moment the interposition is gone they will fall again to where they were before.

And so, the continued pressing or holding together of Universal Substance is the same. What causes the Substance of the earth to gravitate or cohere or hold together? or the Substance of each star the same? or the Substance of each atom the same? What, but that Substance is Spirit, and it thus chooses or wills to clench portions of itself, some in the Shapes of stars and some in the Shapes of atoms. And this Universal Substance is One Spirit, for it holds and moves all those Shapes together in one universal system.

5. "Matter" and "Force" and "Motion" otherwise than as "Spirit-substance" and "Will-pressure" and " Motion" are quite unthinkable.

TRUTH XXII

MOTION CAN HAVE A BEGINNING TO BE AND A CEASING TO BE, UNLIKE SUBSTANCE.

SELF-EVIDENCE OF TRUTH XXII

Can you think how Motion, unlike Substance, can have a beginning to be and a ceasing to be? Yes, why, try and suppose so and you will perceive that, Substance being Spirit, and Motion being the mere shifting of Substance from one position in Space to another position in Space, as the Spirit-Substance acting at will chooses to shift itself from one position in Space to another position in space, or simply, if Spirit-substance at will moves itself or refrains from moving itself, Motion will come into being or go out of being. So therefore, Motion can have a beginning to be and a ceasing to be, unlike Substance: as is quite unthinkable.

COMMENTS ON TRUTH XXII

1. When we consider Substance as Conscious Spirit we plainly perceive that Motion may have a beginning to be and a ceasing to be whensoever the Conscious Spirit chooses to move itself or to refrain from moving itself. So, although we cannot think of Substance or Space or Time as having a beginning to be or a ceasing to be, nevertheless, Motion is different. Motion being but the shifting of Substance from one place to another place, it may therefore have a beginning to be and a ceasing to be, yet not without a cause; and the cause must be external to Motion itself, for not of itself can Motion begin to be or cease to be; but Conscious spirit of itself can begin to move or cease to move. The cause of the beginning or ceasing of Motion then is in Substance: it flows from the very nature of Conscious Spirit.

2. What about Force and Energy? Well, Substance being Spirit the Will-action thereof is the Force that produces or resists the Energy of Motion. You cannot think of any other "force" capable of producing or resisting the Energy of Motion except Will-action. Will-action is the only cause thinkable. So therefore, Spirit being Substance the Will-action therefore is "Force", is the "Force" which produces or resists the "Energy" of Motion: as it is unthinkable otherwise.

3. By analysing this in thought further, we perceive that, Motion, or rather a mass of temporarily-passive Substance in Motion, is carried with the Energy imparted to it by the Will-action which first started or propelled it; and the moment that this Energy which carries it comes in collision with an equal opposing Energy, both the colliding Energies are spent and destroyed and cease to be. They cannot continue to press against each other and so resolve themselves into pressure-force: for the Energy of Motion is not "Will" itself, and cannot "act" like Will. They cannot rebound; the Energies can not: for a rebound is caused by Will-action in Substance holding it together and so making it elastic. The only thinkable result is that they will be stayed, stopped and made to cease to be. And, for more energies to be at the place of collision, "Will" would require to propel or project thither other masses of Substance with Energies, or would require to be there to renew or continue the Energy.

4. Spirit-substance, therefore, by an act of will creates a "pressure-force" which produces the Energy of Motion; and this Motion is destroyed by a similar Counter-Energy. So that from this we see that the universal "Force" of the pressure of Substance against Substance (viz., Cohesion and Gravitation) must be upheld by the continuous Action of Will.

5. Substance being Spirit, its Will-action is the Force that produces or resists the Energy of Motion. Matter has Power because Matter is Spirit.

6. Amongst the variety of words used concerning this reality which is the effect or product of spirit action, viz., Power, it is to be hoped that we will steer clear of confusion by perceiving a well-marked difference always betwixt the strength-power, velocity, force or energy of Actual Motion and that power or Force Proper of the holding together or pressure of Substance against Substance, which causes the apparent attractions.

7. Here would be a splendid Life Work, A "Magnum Opus" as they call it. Yes, it would certainly be worth the while if anyone in these modern days staked their whole life on the elaborating and celebrating the Fact, that "the proof of God's existence is because everything is in Motion." Motion must have its start, or must originate in Mind. Why does a stone fall to the ground? Because of Gravity; because of Attraction. What is Gravity, what is Attraction? Power. What sort of Power? Why, don't you see, must be Will-power. All Power or Forces are what but a pushing together or pressures and must be the outcome of Will-action. They in all their actions cannot cause "Will," but "Will" can cause them. "Two and two make four". It is inconceivable they could otherwise. This must be so. But, "Matter gravitates." It is conceivable however that it could otherwise. It is conceivable that it might not gravitate, or that it might fall up instead of down: and so a cause is required for this phenomenon that "Matter gravitates" ; and that cause must be "Will". However here we see the distinction in respect of Absolute Verity of the two realms, the realm of metaphysics, and the realm of physics.

8. "Will" exists: that in itself is sufficient. What is all the harangue over the word "Free-will" about? The very word "Will" in itself expresses "freedom," without the aid of the superfluous prefix "Free." "Will" exists; there cannot be "Will" except it be "Free-will." And what is all the harangue about "caused or uncaused volition"? "Will" implies Mind, it implies an Intelligent Spirit. You cannot have "Will " without a "Spirit," or " Spirit" without a "Will." The "Conscious Thing" left "Motionless" in "Empty Space" would have a sufficient motive for "Will-Action" from the mere consciousness of itself and of its empty environment if it "chose." There is a reason and it ought to be a good one for every will-action as the agent is responsible: and the reason is the motive to will-action which causes Motion but the reason is not Motion. The reason too is at the spirit's own creation.

9. Will exists. As the agent chooses it can move or not move; it can move right or left, up or down, backwards or forwards as it chooses. Here is an independent "Force." Motion can produce nought but Motion, nay it can only continue Motion, therefore it cannot produce "Will". But "Will" creates motion and destroys it by moving as it chooses. What can create "Will"? All other "Forces" mixing in the most intricate manner could never produce a "Force" like this. Why, this must be uncreated and eternal.

10. Yet, "Will" in itself is not "Force." Also, would it not be better to say "That" which has "Will" is " Free" instead of saying that the "Will" is "Free," for it is self-evident that "Will" means "Freedom."

If "Will" chooses not to cause a Pressure, still the "Will" is there; the will-substance, spirit essence, or matter without Force, so to speak, is there. This substance, essence or matter would have resistance, would prove itself by being impenetrable were it jammed into a corner. It would be indestructible, The manifestation of the action of a " Will" in causing Pressure towards Motion, this is Force. But Matter is conscious: the universe consists of a Substance in movement; that Substance is Mindstuff.

TRUTH XXIII

MOTION HAS A BEGINNING TO BE OR IS CREATED BY WILL-ACTION ALONE.

SELF-EVIDENCE OF TRUTH XXIII

Can you think how conscious beings can move about by their own wills without creating Motion by the effort of their wills? No. Why, try to suppose now the conscious human spirit can apply the touches to the nerve-cords, etc., so as to move at will the organic-engine, vis, the body, in which it is infixed, and you will perceive that, although the organic-engine, vis., the body has Motion in itself apart from the conscious human spirit which tenants it, nevertheless, to guide, direct, or turn that Motion to account, the conscious human spirit must by an effort of will create Motion and apply it in a touch at some or other point. So therefore, Motion has a beginning to be or is created by Will-action alone. As also, it is unthinkable it could otherwise.

COMMENTS ON TRUTH XXIII

1. Already this has been partly self-evidenced and commented upon under the Truth that "Substance is Spirit because it Moves itself into Shapes." And it might be well for the reader to connect what was said upon that point there (See Truth XVII.) with what is said upon this point here.

2. This doctrine of the Spiritual Origin of Force is decisive death to Doubt; Will-Force or Psychic Force stings stoical scepticism terrifically. And yet, Theists as well as Atheists frequently avoid it altogether, or flounder helplessly and ignorantly in it.

3. So now, can you think how anyone can move about at will without creating Motion? No. Anyone may be moved about by imparted Motion; but anyone who would guide or direct at will the course of that imparted Motion, must by effort of will create Motion. And anyone attempting to Move, and being prevented from Moving, creates nevertheless by the effort of attempt a pressure-force against whatever prevents the Motion, and the creation of this pressure-force is equal to or is the same as the creation of Motion. And so, the origin of Force or of Motion lies in Will.

4. "Will" exists. We ourselves are existent "wills". And our wills unquestionably do create a pressure-force towards Motion when they, or rather, when "we" choose.

Pressure-force is not "will" for, how could a mere force will to do anything. It is the Spirit-substance which wills, or which is the "will" in its objective existence so to speak. Do you say that there exists just Matter and force? Very well then, that which wills cannot be mere force; it must be the Matter; therefore, the Matter is Spirit; and as this Spirit matter acts at will, its action is Force.

5. Matter and Force? Why, we cannot think of a pressure-force in Substance at all without it being caused by a "will." A coherency in matter, a pressure-force in itself pressing and without the Substance acting by "will" is ridiculous in the extreme. Further, we cannot think of Force apart from Substance though we can think of Substance without Force: we cannot think of a force pushing through empty space without a substance, yet we can think of a substance occupying a space, without any force or coherency in it and motionless. This then, Conscious Spirit does exist, for we exist. Our conscious spirits must have been evolved or derived in some way from Conscious Spirit: so God exists. God is a Spirit, and over all omnipresent. Spirit must exist in Space, must occupy a space: it is a Substance then. Spirit can act and move voluntarily, or as it chooses; it can move and act at will. Nothing can move and act but a Substance, Spirit then is Substance. And, the acting and moving of Spirit is Force and Energy produced or created by "Will."

6. But what now about the body or organism? And what about the spirit or soul that inhabits it? Well, the body, there it stands, that organic-engine as it is, unmistakably prepared to suit its surrounding, purposely adapted to is external conditions, there it stands like a locomotive engine, steamed up, ready to start. Nevertheless, we plainly perceive that to guide or direct that organic-engine, to move it about at will, the conscious soul or spirit infixed within it must at will create force or Motion so as to apply a touch to one or other of the mainsprings thereof. These

bodies of ours may be looked upon also as temples built and upheld for our benefit by the Great Spirit whose they are. And being entrusted to the care of our spirits it behoves us to make a right use of them, and in no evil way abuse or destroy them. For, how can we expect favours from His hand again, if we perversely waste or throw down these He uprears for us.

7. The body is not the spirit, and the spirit is not the body. By means of the body the spirit becomes en rapport with the environment; and it is difficult to conceive in what means otherwise the spirit could so become, here, in such a surging environment. But the body being given for the spirit there must be a very close connection between both; and that there is, for, agitation of spirit agitates the body in degree, and agitation of body agitates the spirit in degree.

8. Lodged within the brain lies the spirit. The spirit is conscious, as has been said, of different things affecting it, which consciousness of different things is "Thought". Things affecting it, such as Motions coming in through the eye and ear, etc., leave likewise minute changes or impressions upon the walls and fords of its environing encasement, the brain. These minute changes or impressions there left are the memory marks with which it can come in contact, and feel, and infer, and be conscious of their meaning, much in the same way as the blind read with their fingers. The spirit coming in contact with its environing membrane finds there also the nerve-cords by which it can move at will the muscles of the body. And here we perceive how simple the possibility is of the head becoming deranged, while the spirit thus, finding its storehouse in disorder, and the chords of its instruments in confusion, though itself be still a conscious thing possessed of will-action, has nevertheless to submit to be wrongfully considered as of itself insane.

9. What becomes of the spirit or soul during sleep? Why, what but that the conscious soul or spirit-substance lets go its hold of the principal nerve-cords or telegraph-wires in the brain, and pulls or draws itself all in together, and being thus coiled up and not in active contact with its environment, or environing membrane, it has retired and has nothing to be conscious of, and therefore, having nothing to think of does not think. When the body is in an unhealthy condition, or when the spirt is in an anxious state, in either or both cases the spirit in its repose gets disturbed by coming in contact involuntarily and irregularly with some part or other of its environment or environing membrane, and so dreams and sleeplessness occur. And in dreams only part or parts of the spirit is engaged, or rather the whole is but partly engaged with the environing membrane; and of course, too, only part or parts of the environing membrane come in touch with the spirit, and that likewise at random, and hence the confused nature of dreams generally.

10. But the self-evidence of the Truth is that our own human wills do unquestionably create Force or Motion. Our own conscious selves can move a hand or foot whenever we at will choose. And this is accomplished by the conscious selves of us acting at the brain upon the nerve-strings corresponding with hand or foot. If the nerve-strings be broken, or other part of the body not in good working order, the conscious self, soul or spirit may act upon the nerve-strings, but the effect desired will fail to be transmitted on account thus of bad conductors, yet, this may be no fault of the spirit nor weakness of its will-power. This self, this soul, this spirit is one; but taken in combination with its memory-store we may call it "Mind." Some would have us have spirit, soul and body; if by "soul" they mean "Mind" as defined above, let them explain it so; but soul and spirit to my thinking are synonymous terms. In man there is the conscious self, soul or spirit, and there is the memory-store or mind, some markings of which may be in the conscious thing itself, but assuredly

most are just external to it, and there is the body. In health, our bodies bearing records on the brain are most wonderful mechanisms which our spirits use, guide, direct, and turn to account for spirit's sake, which, to do so, our spirits create Force, and introduce it at some point or other, so as to manage those most wonderful machine-mechanisms.

11. We perceive here that the spirits of animals can only manifest their intelligence pretty much as their organisms will allow them so to do. How can animals speak when their vocal organs are so fitted and shaped as to give forth only one characteristic sound? How can animals act as men act, when they have no hands, and when they are at any rate independent of the tailor's art? But, animals think deeply nevertheless, and at a glance can sometimes understand the whole position of circumstances in which at times they happen to be. And, I make bold to say that, animals on the whole display as much intelligence for their own sphere, considering their drawbacks, as men usually do in their sphere with all their reason and advantages.

12. However, How could Substance or any part of it begin to Move except it had a Will? There is a question: let the answer come in silence.

TRUTH XXIV

MOTION HAS A CEASING TO BE OR IS DESTROYED BY DIRECT COLLISION WITH MOTION OR WITH WILL-ACTION.

SELF-EVIDENCE OF TRUTH XXIV

Can you think what would happen otherwise but that Motion would be destroyed or would cease to be by getting into direct collision with Motion or with Will-action?

No. Why, try and suppose what would be the effect as regards Motion when two inelastic bodies meet with equal power of Motion in direct collision with each other in empty space, and you will perceive, that the Motion of each one would just be sufficient to stay or stop the Motion of each other, and the Motions being so stayed or stopped, their energy would be destroyed and would cease to be, for, that the two bodies should continue to press against each other is unthinkable.

Now, try and suppose what would be the effect as regards Motion when two elastic bodies meet with equal power of Motion in direct collision with each other in empty space, and you will perceive, that the Motion of each one, the colliding Motion of each one would be similarly stayed or stopped and made to cease to be, but that the other Motion, the Motion of the elasticity, which would appear in the rebound would be created evidently in the way as follows, viz., in each of the elastic bodies those surface parts which would first receive the brunt of the collision would be forced by the shock some degrees aside from their centre of cohesion with each other, but the colliding Motion immediately being destroyed and its pressure gone, those surface parts would fast come to their centre of cohesion with each other again according to the strength of that pressure-force of cohesion within them, and so doing they would expand to their former places, and this sudden expansion to their original Shapes, of the two surfaces being at the same time so very close together, would throw the bodies back in the rebound; and thus, the rebound would be a new Motion created by the will-action which gave the pressure-force of cohesion in the parts, but the old Motion or Motions which met in collision would be destroyed and would cease to be.

So therefore, Motion has a ceasing to be or is destroyed by direct collision with Motion or with Will-action: As it is unthinkable otherwise.

COMMENTS ON TRUTH XXIV

1. Motion is the mere shifting of Substance from one place to another. When two masses of Substance come into exact, equal collision their shifting from place to place is stopped, and so their Motion is destroyed. If there happen a rebound, the Motion of the rebound is independent on the elasticity of the masses colliding and is therefore new Motion created by the Will-pressure which causes the cohesion or the holding firmly together of the Substance of each of the masses, which cohesion makes the masses elastic.

2. What is Elasticity? It is but a name for a phenomenon. It itself is not the Force which holds the particles of an elastic Substance together; but it is the necessary consequence flowing from a certain opposition taken to this Force of the holding together of Substance. When a mass of Substance undergoes tension, torsion, flexure and compression and yet its parts persist to hold together: here is Elasticity.

When atoms strike each other they are temporarily dis-shaped; and the regaining of their Shapes again by the cohesive Force within them: and their consequent rebound: this is Elasticity. It is unmistakably caused by this Cohesive Force in Substance, this Pressure of Substance against Substance, this Holding together of Substance at Will. Why, think of two definite masses of conscious spirit-substance, think of each one holding firmly in together to itself its own essence or Substance which will thereby take a globular Shape, think of them both thus impinging against each other, and you will perceive the phenomenon of Elasticity. Don't you think that each by collision will be flattened at the point of contact? Don't you think that by each continuing to crush or hold each its own Substance firmly in together to itself their flattened sides will regain their shapes again and give thereby a rebound from each other? Don't you think so? Of course. This then is Elasticity.

3. In the phenomenon of Elasticity, then, we see the Destruction of Motion and the Creation of Motion. Immense and multitudinous are the collisions of Motions happening momentarily throughout the universe, and in all these collisions the colliding Motions with their Energies must be destroyed as they certainly are, for what becomes of them otherwise is unthinkable. Every rebound after impact or collision is new Energy of Motion created by Will-Force: for each rebound is caused by the inherent Force in the Substance drawing or bringing, so to speak, into their original shapes the sides that were dis-shaped by the shock of the collision.

So that, inherent, cohesive Force in drawing the bruised parts of the Substance to their first positions creates a new Motion which appears in the rebound. But the colliding Motion is destroyed, for if it is not, then, it along with the new Motion which is certainly created by the inherent Force which gives Elasticity, must bring the bodies back in the rebound with a double energy of Motion, and so if Motion is not destroyed it must be multiplying at a fearful rate. But it is self-evident that all Motion when stopped or stayed ceases to be and is not. And we see that Elasticity which gives rise to various phenomena of Motion is caused unmistakably by that persistent Force which holds Substance together and which is caused by a Will. So that, it is the persistence of this great, inherent Force, this Will-pressure of Substance against Substance that prevents an entire stand-still in the universe. All the harmonious Motion and Shapes of the universe would cease if the Great Will willed and withdrew His action.

4. If I pull or twist anything elastic and let it go so that it spring, I do not give to it by so doing the inherent, cohesive Force which makes it elastic; that Force is in it before and after my action as strong all the same; I merely bring it into a position or condition wherein it can manifest this Force holding within it. Surely no

one would say that when I Force anything elastic in one direction and let go so that it spring back in the opposite direction—surely no one would say that it is the Identical Force that I put to it in one direction that is rushing back in the opposite direction.

And so the energy of Motion as in heat, light, etc., is totally destroyed when having spent itself in separating atoms or molecules or masses it becomes what has been fancifully called the Energy of Position. Certainly the Position of separation of atoms or of molecules or of masses gives inherent Force an opportunity of creating a new energy of Motion, but this Position has been accomplished at the expense of the first energy of Motion which has spent and destroyed itself completely in doing the work.

So that after the separation of atoms or molecules or masses by the energy of Motion in heat, light, etc., when this energy is spent and destroyed in accomplishing the work, there is a new energy of Motion created when the atoms or molecules or masses rush to their places again.

5. Simply in pure thought, however, can you think what else can ever happen when any two Motions of equal strength meet in exact, direct collision but that each will stop each other and both thereby cease to be? Or when anyone by an act of will puts forth energy, that is, begins or creates Motion, and then by another act of will opposes that Motion with an equal energy so as to arrest it, can you think what can ever happen otherwise, if the Motion is not fed by other sources, but that it will be destroyed and will cease to be? Motion and the Energy thereof is destroyed by thus coming into collision with itself, as it is unthinkable otherwise.

6. Do we not by our wills interfere with and arrest certain Motions in the world around us? Do we not turn rivers out of their course, etc.? This suggests Creation of Motion. But, could not the Almighty by His Will at once arrest all the Motion of His universe? Enormous Force would He require to Create by

His will so to do; but the enormous Force in His universe would be arrested and destroyed by His so doing.

TRUTH XXV

THE UNIVERSAL PRESSURE OF SUBSTANCE AGAINST SUBSTANCE AS IN GRAVITATION OR COHESTON THAT UNIVERSAL FORCE WHICH HOLDS SUBSTANCE TOGETHER, IN THE ATOM AS WELL AS IN THE STAR IS UPHELD, IS CREATED AND DESTROYED BY THE ACTION OF WILL, AS IT IS IN ITSELF SIMPLY WILL-PRESSURE OR WILL-FORCE.

SELF-EVIDENCE OF TRUTH XXV

Can you think how that the universal Pressure of Substance against Substance as in gravitation or cohesion, that universal Force which holds Substance together in the atom as well as in the star can be upheld otherwise than by the action of Will, or be ought else but Will-pressure or Wil-Force? No. Why, try to suppose aught else it may be, or how otherwise it can be upheld, and you will perceive that the Will-action of the Substance itself is capable only and alone, as nought else is, of giving this universal Pressure, this universal Force which is creatable and destructible therefore at Will. So therefore, Universal Force is created and destroyed by the Action of Will: as it is unthinkable otherwise.

COMMENTS ON TRUTH XXV

1.This Force, this Pressure of Substance against Substance, which is just what we call "weight," has been found to have amongst atoms and amongst stars one uniform mode of action generally which makes it thus One Force. This shows the wisdom of the Spirit which gives its action, for acting uniformly generally other spirits can depend upon it as a Law of Nature. Of course, note, that this Force is the Spirit-action itself. It acts somehow in a certain relationship or ratio of Mass and Distance: the larger the masses or quantity of Substance, and the shorter the distances between them, the greater is its effect. Of course, the Shapes of the masses and various cross Motions interfere at times and modify this relative, proportionate mode of action. But on the whole generally, universal Force or Pressure of Substance against Substance acts thus. And, acting thus amongst the stars and planets it has been called the force of Gravitation or Attraction; acting thus amongst the atoms and molecules it has been called the force of Affinity, Cohesion, or Attraction; and acting thus in other circumstances it has received a host of names accordingly, such as Adhesion, Capillary Attraction, etc. This variety of names given to its action under different conditions has caused a great confusion of ideas, making some imagine that there are so many totally distinct Forces; whereas, on the general whole there is just the One Force which acts generally in the uniform manner as stated above.

2. It is an interesting study to unravel the puzzles of the various so-called chemical affinities or attractions, and to perceive how they can all be resolved into what we might call modes of gravity.

3. Here let me protest against the term "Attraction", as well as that of "Repulsion" so-called. If there is an apparent Force of Repulsion it just comes to this that the Force of Attraction so-called is somewhere the cause of it. There is just one Force always, and that Force is a Force Pushing. But what is meant by Attraction? How can anything "Attract" or "draw in" an object without getting a force round behind the object, and thus pushing or pressing it in? Say, is not Pressure-Force the proper term? And what else can cause Pressure-Force but "Will"? Most grievous and fatal has been the mistake in giving to this

tendency of Substance to aggregate together that most highly objectionable name of "Attraction." But ask what "Attraction" is and you will somewhat surprise the same number who thought they knew all about it. Some will say that "Attraction" acts through vacuum, that through actual empty space the worlds mutually "attract" each other: and it is needless to tell such that if the worlds thus (?) affect each other there must be then some tangible connection somewhere betwixt them. In fact, the idea of "Attraction" as a cause, or as having even any existence at all, is one of the most odious and idiotic that has ever blasted the brains of men. Just think upon it! "Every mass attracts every other mass in the universe:" what a hideous amount of feelers each mass must throw out then, for there is no other way to attract but to throw out feelers to other masses and thereby affect them. The term "Attraction" is immensely misleading. Universal Pressure-Force is a better term; it is suggestive too of its nature; it suggests a something which gives the Pressure, and thus leads at once to Will-action somewhere.

4. Now, this Universal Pressure-Force, tending continually as it does to press in the smaller masses to the larger masses, will ultimately assemble all matter into one immense mass—suns falling into suns, etc. But then, though the Shapes of suns and worlds disappear, the vigour of the Eternal Spirit still remains. It is the Force of His Action that is seen in the very crash and crush of worlds. The very holding tight together of the Substance of the so-called dead suns is immense evidence of strong life in nature. Mind and Will is behind all Force; and Spirit never can lose its power: the very existence of Spirit is the possibility of Power-Oh Everlasting God!

5. Look at this! I clench both my hands separately; the pressure or cohesion in both is caused by my single will: so the Single Will of the Great Spirit gives the pressure or cohesion of the clenched substance, so to speak, of each separate atom—Behold the fingers

of the Almighty! But further, I bring my clenched hands and press them both firm together; and this firm holding of them both together is still caused by my single Will: so the Single Will of the Great Spirit presses the clenched atoms together, thus making the chemical molecule. But still further, while keeping each of my hands tightly clenched, and while still keeping them both firmly pressing together, I press the whole firmly down upon the top of my desk or table: here now is a third pressure-force, and it also is caused by my single will: so the Single Will of the Great Spirit presses the molecules together actual into larger masses, and so on. This is actual practical experiment and demonstration to show that the coherency of each atom, and the so-called chemical attraction or affinity of atom for atom, and then the gravitating of the whole together is caused by the One Great Will of the Great Spirit. Here in this illustration are forces within forces, and all the product of my one will. So the forces within forces in the great universe are unmistakeably, and cannot be anything else but the product of the Great Will. Why, consider the cuttle-fish; consider its numerous tentacles, along the under surface of each of which it has a multitude of suckers; with its single individual will it can cause a suction or pressure in each, in some, or in all at once of these suckers: and this is but an organism, consider what a mass of pure, fluid, Spirit-Substance might do in comparison.

6. Considering Universal Substance then as One Vast Spirit Essence capable of voluntary action or movement, as it certainly is: for God is a Spirit, and His Spirit is everywhere, and Spirit Moves and acts, and nothing can Move and act but a Substance. Considering Universal Substance thus, we will perceive that by its Will-action it will be able to hold portions of itself rigid and firm and solid, and leave other portions of itself loose and fluid and pliable. We will perceive further that the fluid portions will be subject to various accidental agitations on account of the movements of the solid parts within them, and that these

accidental agitations in the fluid parts will again re-act back and give also chance Motions to the solid parts.

From this view we can easily distinguish two forms of Power, viz., The Power of the Holding together of Substance, and The Power of Actual Motion.

7. Now, in the Universe as it is, which we know can assume either a solid, liquid or gaseous condition, we actually have those two great divisions of Power: first, the Force of the Holding together of Substance, and second, the Energy of Actual Motion.

To the First belong all the so-called Attractions or Forces of Gravitation, of Cohesion, of Chemical Affinity, etc., which so-called Attractions or Forces are all modes of the Holding together of Substance as it acts under different conditions in the infinitely great or little. To the Second belong all the so-called Energies of Light, Heat, Electricity, Sound, etc., revolutions of stars and planets, surgings and rollings of oceans and rivers whirling and swaying of winds, etc., which so-called Energies, etc., are all modes of Actual Motion as it takes place under different conditions in the infinitely great or little.

8. Now note, the Power of Actual Motion is transmutable through the various phases of Actual Motion, as for instance, Light into Heat, Heat into Electricity, Electricity into Light, Sound, etc. But this Power of Actual Motion is not transmutable into the Power of the continuous Holding together of Substance: for, although in collisions it may give a Pressure of Substance against Substance, and therefore for the time being a temporary Holding together of Substance, yet, it is only temporary, as all collisions are the very destruction of this Power of Actual Motion. And, as has been shown before on Elasticity, that out of collisions Actual Motion arises anew, being produced therefrom by the Power of the Holding together of Substance, therefore, instead of the Power of Actual Motion being transmutable into the Power of the Holding together of Substance, it is the

Power of the Holding together of Substance which creates and continues the Power of Actual Motion. Why, though chemical molecules by a Heat, Light, or Electric surge be shattered into their separate atoms, the formation of those atoms into molecules again is not caused by the Heat, Light, or Electric Surge that separated them, but by that great Power of the Pressure of Substance against Substance, that great power of the Holding together of Substance. And when, by the formation of the atoms into molecules again, a Heat, Light, or Electric Surge is set up, the Surge is a new Actual Motion created by that Power which gives the molecular formation.

9. What now is the cause of this Power of the Holding together of Substance, this Power of the Pressure of Substance against Substance, which is the creator and upholder of the Power or Energy of Actual Motion by giving Elasticity to the particles of Substance and thereby handing on Actual Motion from one particle to another, and yet not in the least degree lessening its own Power though giving forth that of Actual Motion-what is its cause? Well, we ourselves have Wills; and at Will we can cause a Pressure of Substance against Substance, or Holding together of Substance by our action. And it is utterly inconceivable or unthinkable that aught else can cause a Pressure together or a Holding together of Substance except Will.

Therefore, This great Power must be caused by a Great Will. And as the Great Universal Spirit must be a Great Universal Substance having the Power of Will-action, so the Great Universal Substance proves itself to be a Great Universal Spirit by its Power of Holding itself together. This Holding together of Substance, this Pressure of Substance against Substance is Will-action, Will-Pressure or Will force; for there is not in all Being or Existence aught else capable of Holding Substance together but its own actual Will-action, Will-pressure or Will-force. And as this Great Force though acting under different conditions amongst atoms and stars is nevertheless just One Force, the Great Will which is its cause is but One. The various moving atoms are controlled by One Will, for were they moving by wills of their own how could they know how to move in the universal harmony in which they do move? When I clench my hands there are not two separate wills in each hand; my will clenches them both. God, by His Will, has the Substance of Himself, clenched firmly, rigidly in atoms and in stars.

10. All Motions are traceable to Will-Pressure. Those wheels whirling on our streets are in Motion because the cars are in Motion: the cars are in Motion because the horses' feet are in Motion: the horses' feet are in Motion because their muscles are in Motion: the muscles are in Motion because of the nerve strings being pressed or acted upon by the wills of the horses. And so the whirling of the wheels on our streets is traceable to will-pressure. Again, those wheels of machinery whirring in our riverside factories are in Motion because the great water-wheel is in Motion: the great water-wheel is in Motion because the river is in Motion: and the river is in Motion because of what we call Gravitation—that great universal Pressure of Substance against Substance or Holding together of Substance, which must be caused by, or be actually will-action.

And so, the whirring of the wheels of machinery in our river-side factories is traceable to will-pressure. Once more, of that multitudinous Motion of swaying and shaking leaves and branches, the direct cause is the Wind: the Wind is the air in Motion, the direct cause of which is Heat: Heat is the luminiferous ether in a surge of Motion, the direct cause of which is the colliding of the chemical atoms and molecules which float in the ether: and the colliding of the atoms and molecules together is caused by what is called Attraction or Affinity—that great universal Pressure of Substance against Substance or Holding together of Substance which must be caused by, or be actually Will-action.

And so, that multitudinous Motion of swaying and shaking leaves and branches is traceable to Will-pressure. Also, Motion of all steam-power machinery is traceable as in the last case through Heat down to atomic Will-pressure. Every Motion in the universe, if traced, will be found to originate in Will-pressure or Will. Will is the source of Force or Motion.

11. Having traced Motions to their source, let us now trace Motions from their source. Take the throwing of a stone: The thrower wills to do so, and his "will" acts on the nerve-strings of the brain, these act on the muscles of the arm and hand, and the stone thereby is thrown through the air moving billions of air particles in its course. It drops into a lake of water suppose, and its plunge causes innumerable ripples and vibrations, these act and re-act, and the tremor is almost universal—in fact, scientists do assert that is does affect the whole material universe.

And so the source of this Motion was in "Will." But, when a stone is thrown, where goes all its created Motion? Well, in passing through the elastic air and the elastic ether within the air, it gives rise to a multitudinous zig-zag Motions or agitations therein, on account of the elasticity of these media, and Sound, Heat, Electricity, and other such Motions may be produced by it, and perhaps Light, if the stone strike and produce sparks over some rock edge, and if it fall into water, every molecule of the water receives its share of the agitation. The stone being opposed and oppressed by the friction, etc., ceases to move and so comes to rest; but the zig-zag Motions which it produced in the path it travelled-what of them? They—acting and reacting and vibrating, and that too on account of the elasticity, backwards and forwards upon themselves—what of them? Well, they to by acting and reacting and vibrating backwards and forwards upon themselves cease to move, and so come to rest also, or to the state called "statical equilibrium," which is simply the state of Motion destroyed or ceased to be. For, say the scientists, "there exists a tendency to equilibrium": well then, when all the universe "statically balances," or is "in equilibrio," what will break that equilibrium? Answer-Will-Action or Will-Force.

12. But let us now behold the Action of the Great Spirit, and the effects and purposes thereof taking Shape, and all the consequent Motion of the universe flowing from His Great Will. Let us go back to "In the beginning," and here we have God, The Great Spirit-essence, The Great Spirit-substance, filling the calm of Space alone.

He wills that the Creation be, and His Spirit-substance or Spirit-essence He moves, and in this uniform Spirit-essence or Substance of God a multitudinous nonillion of nonillions of infinitesimal points become firm and rigid by His Will-pressure or Force, and these points constitute the elastic particles of the luminiferous ether which vibrates Light.

Now, before becoming thorough rigid and fixed, a multitudinous million of millions of these luminiferous particles are pressed together in various quantities into various groups which become firm and rigid, and which become the chemical atoms, having different Shapes by mutual pressure against each other while forming, and having different weights according to the quantity of Substance they contain. Then, those chemical atoms fall or press together into chemical molecules, and so doing give rise to a terrible heat surge, as well as light in the ether, and here we have a vast vapour-cloud of chemical elements and compounds, the material for stellar, solar and world systems. And so God said "Let there be Light"; and there was Light. This luminous vapour-cloud still pressing all round in together upon itself begins under the sway of the Great Will to sway round its centre or axis and to revolve; and as various parts of it begin to cool, those various parts press or condense from vapour into liquid, and here we have globes of liquid matter pressing and swaying with the general current round a common centre.

But the vapour surrounding each of these globes and pressing all round in upon them begins likewise under the guiding sway of the Great Will to sway around them and to revolve; thus forming sub-centres which still revolve around the great common centre. In the vapour swaying around these sub-centres, again, other portions press or condense into liquid globules; and thus systems are formed which revolve around the one, great, common centre. And this process goes on, system being formed or shaped within system, wheel within wheel, till we have this great universe of worlds with its Multitudinous Motion flowing thus directly from the Will-action of the Great Spirit-substance of God who is actually All in All. This is the famous "Nebular Hypothesis" which makes the 1st chapter of Genesis a miracle to modern times. "In the beginning God" (was) (He) "created the heavens and the earth" (a mere system of Shapes); "and the earth was without form and void" (that is, without shape, non-extant), and darkness was upon the face of the deep" (the deep of Space); "and the Spirit of God Moved upon the face of the waters" (that is, upon the face of the fluid essence filling Space). "And God said, Let there be Light, and there was Light, and God saw the Light that it was good." (He willed it to be and then wrought it out). "And God divided the Light from the darkness" (by the taking Shape of the worlds, and by their diurnal revolutions). All this is but the First Period or Day's work. The Second Day's work is the clearing of the firmament or atmosphere: upon the surface of each molten world a crust forms, and as it cools the watery vapour of the surrounding atmosphere condenses thereon and covers with water from pole to pole. The Third Day's work is the gathering the waters together into one place that the dry land appear and bring forth grass and herb: and so, the internal fires and other causes upheave the crust at various places, and the waters press thereby into the hollows, and vegetation appears at length upon the dry land. The Fourth Day's work is the fixing of the great lights in the sky to rule over the day and night: and so, by this period the neighbouring worlds in their process of development have arrived at their proper magnitude, and the spaces betwixt and the atmosphere are sufficiently cleared to admit of the full inflow of their (the sun and moon's, etc.) influences. The Fifth and Sixth Day's work is the evolution or creation of the various forms of life in the sea, air, and land, and finally man: and so, as the conditions are at length favourable life begins to abound and in the order of development at last, man. And thus the Source of all this scene of things is in the Will of God.

13. So much for the process constantly upholds of the Almighty's purpose in His universe which He constantly upholds. But let this be noted that howsoever the forces or energies after being let loose in the universe may work in causing gravity or cohesion, nevertheless, all Force or Energy must originate or be created by the Action of the Will of Spirit.

14. How does the Great Spirit work in the universe? He, by His Will-action, causes the Pressure, causes the Force or Energy; and though His mode of affecting His purpose may be by taking advantage of the fact in the general aggregation of matter together that masses by shielding each other from the general Energy beating about them are thus pushed together, nevertheless, the Origin of Force and Energy is in the action of His Will, for how could it otherwise? And as Spirit has the Power to Act, it must be able then to hold its own Substance together, and guide, direct, and turn to account the drifting at random of escaped Energies.

15. The cause of the continuous Force or Pressure of Substance against Substance is not in Motion; for, to think of two or more atoms all meeting each other in collision at a certain point, and then remaining there pressing against each other after the collision by virtue of the Force of Motion which brought them

together in collision: this is both ridiculous in its very idea as well as in its consequences. If Motion acted thus there could never be Elasticity.

Also, if this Force or Pressure of Substance against Substance were caused, say, by the beating of Motion on all sides of masses of matter with the exception of those shaded sides which would be next each other so that the masses of matter would be thus pressed together, nevertheless, the origin of the continued beating of the external Motion would have to be accounted for, and could only be accounted for by being the product of Will-Action somewhere. In fact, the universal Pressure of Substance against Substance is plainly perceived to be the grasp of God.

16. Motion nor Force nor Spirit can be thought of apart from Substance. They imply respectively a something moving, a something pressing, a something that can act, which something must be a Substance.

17. Now, anyone placed at rest away out in absolute Space somewhere in the midst of ether, air or water, could easily move out of position by beating his environment in one direction and so pushing himself on in the opposite direction. But were anyone placed at rest away out in empty, absolute Space somewhere, how could that one shift his position? By striking out into the vacuity with a part of himself then nothing would resist the stroke, and unless he himself counteracted it the force of it would tug him on entire in the direction which was struck if he held himself whole together. This is interesting as showing how spirits can Move through empty Space. At any rate, Spirits could bridge Space by elongating themselves.

18. Note the difference betwixt a body moving through ether, air or water and continuing itself in Motion therein by the constant effort of its will, and a body moving therein, but being projected into Motion passively by the force of some external will.

Also, Note that a body moving through empty Space does not require to do so at the continuous effort of its will. (Kinetics and Kinematics forever!) A mass of Substance might move through empty Space forever when once set a moving should it never come in collision. The whole universal mass of Substance, if it be finite, may be so moving. Yet, nevertheless, a sudden throw of Will-Force within Substance so moving could alter its course or could be made to turn it directly back from the direction it was going. Any mass of Substance moving through empty, absolute Space and then at length coming against a solitary, stationary and passive mass, what would be the result? Well, we can think of the solitary, stationery mass as existing in either of two degrees of passivity, first, passive as a whole to its Motion in absolute Space but holding its Substance firm together by its inherent will-force, and second, passive absolutely not only in one whole as above but to all parts of its Substance having no firmness or coherency in the most infinitesimal particle thereof. In the first case whatever pushed against it at any part would push it on as a whole; in the second case only the part that was pushed against would be pushed on in front of the impinging body. But in either case, although the Shapes of the colliding masses might be altered, they would both together be moved on with the original momentum, not one iota less.

19. But to return to the old subject of Force and Motion, shall we call the former Pressure of Substance against Substance and the latter Energy of Actual Motion? Well, Let be so, but note this well that the Energy of Actual Motion shows itself always in the universe to be produced from the Force of pressure of Substance against Substance or from direct Will-Action.

20. To conclude, Motion or the mere shifting of Substance is created by direct will-action or from will-pressure, and is destroyed by coming into direct collision with equal motion or from being adequately opposed: For, that conscious beings can

move and act at will without creating Motion by effort of their wills, or that that Force, that universal Pressure of Substance against Substance, which holds the universe together and gives harmonious Motion to its parts, can be aught else but Will-pressure, or that that Will-pressure could otherwise but be destroyed by coming into direct collision with equal Motion, is quite unthinkable.

SHAPES

TRUTH XXVI

SHAPES ARE NEITHER TIME NOR SPACE NOR SUBSTANCE NOR MOTION, BUT SIMPLY SHAPES.

SELF-EVIDENCE OF TRUTH XXVI

Can you think of mere Shapes as being Time or Space or Substance or Motion? No. Why, try to suppose mere Shapes as being Substance, and you will perceive, that although Substance must always have some Shape or Shapes, nevertheless Substance itself is not the Shape or Shapes. So mere Shapes have no comparison to aught but themselves, and cannot be defined in terms of aught but themselves, and therefore Shapes are simply Shapes.

COMMENTS ON TRUTH XXVI

1. Here comes the fifth and last great reality of Being or Existence, viz., Shapes. A clear conception of this department of Being or Existence gives an almost perfect grasp of the universe. It is remarkable that the people have heard much about Time and Space, Substance and Motion, and yet little or nothing about shapes; while on the very face of things it is evident to all who will but look at it, that Shapes, along with Time, Space, Substance, and Motion, are absolutely necessary to the completion of the Entire Total of Being or Existence. It is all the more remarkable on account of the fact that Shapes, mere Shapes of Substance (though scarcely ever looked at in that light) are, nevertheless, absorbing almost the entire attention of the people that they seldom or even ever think of Time, Space, Substance, and Motion, and that they seldom or ever think of

the Fact that it is alone with mere transitory Shapes of Substance that their attention is being absorbed. To mere transitory Shapes of Substance, which might crumble away, dissolve and disappear at any moment of Time they give names, and these are pre-eminently The Things with them, The Things upon which they set their affections and build.

They look so closely upon the Shapes of Substance, and so overlook the Substance itself, that they come to think that the Substance is nothing, or that it is as passive and unconscious as the Shapes, or that it exists merely for the sake of the Shapes. They think they are defining Substance when they name the Shapes or Shape or appearances it presents, and the manner in which it moves or presses: and so when they define the Shapes or Shape and the mode of motion of these, they think that they do analyse Substance itself. By a dull, dim, careless reason, and a highly reprehensible want of intellectual penetration and abstractive power, they do mingle and confuse Shapes and Substance together, and think they know what Substance is when they know what its Shape or Shapes are.

2. Substance is just One. It's the "That" that exists in Space. It is itself. It must have a Shape: but it may throw itself into an infinite variety of Shape. It may dissolve the shapes in which it now is in and then throw itself into an infinite variety of other Shapes again.

3. The fact is we never see substance itself. We only see the shapes into which substance throws itself. The objects which light reveals to us are merely shapes of things. The waves of light dash there against a something which is held in a certain shape, and which says to them "thus far and no farther;" They are reflected back to our eyes, and they tell us of a something being there, and they tell us of the Shape that that something happens to be in at the time, but they do not tell us what that something is.

We even do not, strictly speaking, see the colour of any object: for colour does not belong to any object. The colour reflected from any object does not come out of the object, but is the particular light-vibrations which the object will not, so to speak, receive, and therefore repels back. The Shapes of Things are all that in reality we can see. (Vide II. Cor. IV. 18.)

TRUTH XXVII

STARS, CLOUDS, HILLS, TREES, BODIES, STONES, ATOMS, ETC., ARE ACTUALLY NOT SUBSTANCE BUT SHAPES.

SELF-EVIDENCE OF TRUTH XXVII

Can you think how stars, clouds, hills, trees, bodies, stones, atoms, etc are actually not substance but shapes? Yes. Why, try to suppose now a star, a cloud, a hill, a tree, a body, a stone, or an atom, and you will perceive that it is not the substance you give the name of "star," "cloud," "hill," "tree," "body," "stone" or "atom," but to the Shape or Shapes in which the Substance is. So therefore, stars, clouds, hills, trees, bodies, stones, atoms, etc., are actually not Substance but Shapes: as is quite thinkable.

COMMENTS ON TRUTH XXVII

1. Truly, such names as "Stars", "Clouds", "Hills", "Trees", "Bodies", "Stones", "Atoms", etc., but names given to certain shapes. Almost all that we have been in the habit of calling things are after all but mere Shapes.

2. As a simple example take this desk, or this table, or this chair. You see that table there, now, what is it that we call "Table"? Very plainly indeed it is not the Substance that we call "Table", but the

Shape into which the Substance is cast. That particular Shape we call a Table. Were a joiner to come and break it down and form it into a chair, then would a chair be created, but where would the Table have gone? It would have disappeared; It would have been totally destroyed. The chair again, what we call "Chair" would have the same precarious existence, that of a mere shape, and be liable to lose its Shape and therefore cease to be a chair, as what we call "Chair" is actually just a certain shape. A box again might be Shaped therefrom, But, the underlying Substance remains.

3. So, the Earth itself is but a mere Shape, a globe. Pre-existent Substance rolling itself up or being rolled up has become rigid in that Shape.

But, says Shakespeare :—

"The cloud-capped towers, the gorgeous palaces,

The solemn temples, the great globe itself,

Yea, all that it inherit, shall dissolve,

And,

Leave not a wrack behind."

He ought to have said, — "Leave not a Shape behind."

4. In the beginning God created the earth and the heavens unmistakeably, but the earth and the heavens are a mere system of shapes. All objects from stars and systems to atoms and molecules with the exception of the substance itself but media shapes.

5. Here now is the test and strength of your metaphysical brains. It is very simple indeed, yet very profound. So simple indeed and so profound indeed that it has been overlooked by the many and scarcely ever noticed by the few. Have you ever heard mentioned, "the Abstraction of Shapes from Substance"? It is not to the Substance thereof that we give the names of these

so-called things, but the so-called things to which we give names are certain Shapes into which the Substance is cast. Grasp this, and you grasp the idea of the universe, you grasp the idea that substance is "One".

6. We might have wood, but wood of itself would neither be table, chair, nor box, until the table, chair, or box-shapes were respectively imposed upon it; nor even then would the wood be called table, chair, or box, but the names table, chair, and box would refer to the particular Shapes respectively.

Now then are you thinking that the wood is Substance? The wood is not Substance; but "wood" is a name given to a particular texture of Substance. You never before knew what Substance was in itself; all your definitions of it were but names describing certain peculiar Shapes or Shapings of it: As we shall see in our next.

TRUTH XXVIII

WOOD, STONE, WATER, AIR, THE CHEMICAL ELEMENTS, THE LUMINIFEROUS ETHER, ETC., ARE NOT DIFFERENT SUBSTANCES, BUT MERELY DIFFERENT CONGLOMERATE AGGREGATES OF DIFFERENT INFINITESIMAL SHAPES.

SELF-EVIDENCE OF TRUTH XXVIII

Can you think how wood, stone, water, air, the chemical elements, the luminiferous ether, etc., are not different Substances but merely different conglomerate aggregates of different infinitesimal shapes? Yes. Why, try to suppose now what constitutes wood, stone, air, water, the chemical elements, the luminiferous ether, etc., and you will perceive that the difference of each lies in the differently Shaped ultimate particles of each and that it is to the conglomerate aggregations respectively of such ultimate particles that we give such names as "wood," "stone," "water," "air," "the chemical elements," "the luminiferous ether," etc. So therefore wood, stone, water, air, the chemical elements, the luminiferous ether, etc., are not different Substances, but merely different conglomerate aggregates of different infinitesimal Shapes: As is quite thinkable.

COMMENTS ON TRUTH XXVIII

1. Stars, clouds, hills, trees, etc., may be looked upon as Simple Shapes; while wood, stone, water, air, etc., may be looked upon as Compound or Complex Shapes.

2. What now makes wood, wood, and what now makes stone, stone? Well, what we call "Wood" is a conglomerate aggregation or mass of variously-shaped vegetable cells intermixed with vegetable vessels, etc. What we call "Stone" is generally a conglomerate aggregation or mass of variously-shaped little hard solid particles, intermixed with minute crystals, etc. Now, the cells of the Wood and the solid particles of the Stone are Shapes, Simple Shapes in themselves, having Substance underlying, or having still smaller Shapes of Substance underlying.

3. Water, what we call "Water," is the aggregation of Molecular-Shapes made each of one Oxygen atom and two Hydrogen atoms. Such three-atomed Molecular-Shapes aggregating together make what we call "Water". They do not aggregate tight together but roll freely over each other. When they do aggregate tight together and keep fixed places, then strictly speaking it is not "water" that we have, but that that we call "Ice." Air, what we call "Air" is the aggregation together of various Molecular-Shapes, but in a looser manner, or in a manner wider apart from each other than in Water, and therefore they roll still more freely over an around each other.

4. Every Mass-Shape can be split by chemistry into its multitudinous Molecular-Shapes, and those again into them minute Atomic-Shapes, but chemistry bows down in silence before the Substance that underlies and holds itself together in the Atomic-Shapes.

5. Chemistry splits all forms of Substance into atoms; of which atoms it finds over seventy different sorts: which different sorts are called "Chemical Elements." The Hydrogen element consists of the lightest atoms, while the Oxygen element consists of atoms sixteen times heavier. Now, although commonly understood, the chief distinguishing characteristic of each element is its weight, nevertheless, just as important are its atomic shapes. For it is evident that atoms of similar weights, but of different Shapes, would have different properties, and would therefore make different elements. For example, let us take a mass or volume of any single element: we define it to be such and such an element on account of certain properties it manifests; but let us now suppose that every atom it contains were halved or quartered or broken into parts of any degree, and we will then very plainly conceive, and any theoretic chemist will as plainly see, that in either of these reduced conditions it could not be the same element it was before for it would manifest different properties entirely, and be there for an altogether new element. And so the elementary nature of the elements depends as much on the ultimate shapes as on the ultimate weights. And as we consider that the ultimate weights depend upon the amount more or less of substance crushed within the atomic volumes, then the elementary nature of the elements totally depends upon the ultimate Shapes.

6. Now the luminiferous Ether fluid in which all the chemical atoms are immersed, being elastic it must be an aggregation of terrifically minute, definitely Shaped (perhaps spherical) elastic-particles: the elasticity of the particles being on account of

the Substance of each particle pressing all round in upon a centre in itself, that is, holding all itself together. These ether-particles are the most ultimate particles to our knowledge, the minutest Shapes that science can reveal to us.

7. But, further, may there not be, or must there not be a pure fluid Substance in which all the ether-particles are immersed? And may not or must not such a Substance be an actual pure fluid, not composed of any ultimate, rigid, elastic particle-Shapes however minute, but a pure fluid infinitesimally fluid, infinitesimally pliable, infinitesimally movable, as we conceive All Substance to be before cohering into particles, or into atoms, for all Substance is Spirit-Substance?

TRUTH XXIX

SHAPES CAN HAVE A BEGINNING TO BE AND A CEASING TO BE, UNLIKE SUBSTANCE.

SELF-EVIDENCE OF TRUTH XXIX

Can you think how Shapes, unlike Substance, can have a beginning to be and a ceasing to be? Yes. Why, try and suppose so and you will perceive that when Substance throws itself or is thrown into some one particular Shape that particular Shape has its beginning to be, and it continues to be so long as the Substance holds itself or is allowed to be held in that particular Shape, and that particular Shape ceases to be when the Substance throws itself or is thrown into another Shape. So therefore, Shapes can have a beginning to be and a ceasing to be, unlike Substance: As is quite thinkable.

COMMENTS ON TRUTH XXIX

1. Out of the universal Substance new Shapes are continually appearing and old ones disappearing.

2. Were the universal Pressure of Substance against Substance withdrawn or withheld by the Great Will-Power, all the Shapes of the universe, simple or complex, minute or immense, would evanish and the Eternal Substance or Spirit-Essence, fluid to its infinitesimal depths, would alone remain. The Eternal Essence or Substance then could not be said to be composed of ultimate units as the luminiferous ether is, or if it could, then the units themselves would be fluid specks, and the units of those units the same, and, so on to infinity, infinitely fluid. And to finite spirits moving in the midst thereof, to them it would seem as if moving in the midst of vacuum.

3. The Eternal Substance is not composed of eternal, ultimate particles: the ultimate particles begin to be by Will-pressure. Neither can there be any inelastic, ultimate, rigid particles; for however minute any rigid particle may be, it becomes rigid or firm by virtue of all its Substance pressing all round in together en masse upon itself or towards the centre of itself, and this guarantees its elasticity. No particle out of the depths, however minute, could become rigid and firm otherwise. Therefore, there is no inelastic, rigid particle; for particles of rigid Substance being so formed must be elastic.

4. Shapes like motions then originate out of Will-action. When opposing portions of Substance by the Will-power of the Substance press together or against each other, a Shape begins to be. The fallacious idea now that God created the world out of nothing is here unriddled: for the world is a mere, huge Shape composed of smaller Shapes, all which His Power brought into being. "In the beginning God created the heavens and the earth; and the earth was without form and void" (that is, without Shape its Substance was, and therefore void of coherency, and thus

actually vacant and nonextant,) "and darkness was upon the face of the deep;" (the deep of Space.) "And the Spirit of God Moved upon the face of the waters," (of fluid Eternal Essence.) "And God said, 'Let there be light,' and there was light." The luminiferous particle Shapes began to be at His Will; the Eternal Essence or Substance concreted, condensed or pressed together and the world arose.

5. Shapes disappear and cease to be when any external force separates the compressing portions, or when the Substance chooses of itself to stay the pressure in its opposing portions. The imagery in the Apocalypse of the heavens and earth departing as a scroll when it is rolled together, is excessively sublime in this consideration, as also that of a new heaven and a new earth, the former things being passed away. In actual reality the visible universe exists and is upheld by the Will of God. "He upholds all things by the word of His power."

6. Simply, that Shapes or Forms have not a beginning to be and not a ceasing to be when Substance assumes whatever Shapes it chooses, is quite unthinkable. When the potter moulds the clay into a certain Shape, that certain Shape begins then to be, and it ceases to be when by any cause whatsoever it becomes dis-shaped. Even were Substance composed of ultimate, inelastic, rigid particles we could think of it moving itself, or at least, of it being moved out of one large, irregular mass into spheres or cubes or any particular Shape, and from thence again moving itself, or at least, being moved back into one, large, irregular mass. And so we can think of Shapes having a beginning to be and a ceasing to be, but we cannot think so of Substance itself.

TRUTH XXX

SHAPES INTO WHICH SUBSTANCE MOVES ITSELF, AND IN WHICH IT HOLDS ITSELF, ARE THE MANIFESTATIONS OF MIND.

SELF-EVIDENCE OF TRUTH XXX

Can you think how Shapes into which Substance moves itself, and in which it holds itself, are the manifestations of mind. Why, try to suppose how otherwise conscious being could better manifest its mind to others then by thus designing itself into certain Shapes, and you will then perceive the meaning why the glorious Shapes of the creation are silently and grandly held up before the gaze. So therefore, Shapes into which Substance moves itself, and in which it holds itself, of the manifestations of mind: As it is unthinkable what could otherwise.

COMMENTS ON TRUTH XXX

1. There are the Shapes of the organic creation, and there are the Shapes of the inorganic creation, from both which immense intelligent design blazes forth.

2. Excessively interesting and instructive are the Shapes of the Organic creation. Almost infinite is the enormous variety of plants and animals. Here is scope for rumination and delight: Shapes in the forest, Shapes in the sea; insect Shapes; Shapes of leaves; What evident design in all! Said the Duke of Argyll to the great Darwin—"It is impossible to look at these without seeing that they are the effect and the expression of Mind." Said the great Darwin to the Duke of Argyll — "Well, that often comes over me with overwhelming force, but at other times it seems to go away." —Vide "What is Science" in Good Words for April, 1885.

Excessively sublime, beautiful and wonderful are the Shapes of the Inorganic creation. Astronomy's awful range of planets and suns and systems; Chemistry's immeasurable swarm of atoms and complex molecules and crystals; Geology's and Geography's masses, irregular but romantic and thought inspiring: What an immensity of Design!

3. Paley, chiefly from the Design which lies in the Organic Shapes, drew his argument for a Deity. But greater argument for a Deity can now be drawn from the Design which lies in the Inorganic order of Shapes. The Organic Shapes are sometimes modified and marred by the finite spirits encased within them (though even this modifying and marring is nevertheless the effect and tracings of mind—finite mind,) but the Inorganic Shapes are directly for the most part the Design and Work of God; and though they be sometimes modified and marred by finite spirits too, yet that is plainly apparent on the surface and can be distinguished. Organic Evolution is the co-working of the Great Spirit with finite spirits to Shape out adaptable, perfect organisms. The Great Spirit must give and make the appropriate solid atoms for the finite spirits to build about themselves bodies. But do the finite spirits with the atoms given build themselves bodies? It is evident that they aid only in the work, and their aid is sometimes destructive and hindersome. The great glory of the work belongs to the Great Spirit. Supposing even that we granted that it was altogether the work of the finite spirits themselves, that they gradually through ages by the slow process of gradually adapting their organisms to their surroundings built at last perfect organisms about themselves: nevertheless this would still be the work, "the effect and expression of" Mind; there is no getting away from that. How desperately blind and foolish were the sceptics who prated about "Evolution!" Why, " Design" blazes forth in "Evolution." The Great Spirit upholds these bodies of ours in Shape; and not we ourselves, I scarce need say so.

4. In the Inorganic order of Shapes, chiefly those of the chemical atoms and molecules, awful design bursts forth. The atoms constituting the chemical elements are the foundation stones of the mighty universe, and they have been hewn out or shaped beforehand with that vast superstructure in view. There are seventy or more varieties of atoms, which varieties are called "Elements", and each variety is in its place and necessary for the vast superstructure of the universe. And I may venture to say that if a single one of these varieties were awanting, or different from what it is, there would be a hitch in the great superstructure of this universe. Sceptical evolutionist, where wast thou when God laid the foundations of the earth? Maybe thy spirit was absorbed in His and helped thus to plan beforehand the universe that was to be. I noted a child once putting together and building up a structure with a definite number of peculiar shaped pieces of wood. Each piece had its own Shape, which was made so that it could only be fitted in into one place or position with the others. And when each piece was put into its proper relative place or position, it was found to be flush so far with the other pieces, and the entire result was a superb, model mansion. Any one piece put into its wrong place, or put out of its place, put all the others wrong in their relations, and the result aimed at could never be attained.

I perceived the necessity there was of each piece being Shaped aright, and I perceived that each piece could only have been Shaped aright by the maker thereof having had in view the whole result. And so, God, when He Shaped the atoms, had in view the result of the universe entire. None but a wilfully blind observer can fail to see the deep design in the Shapes or weights of the atoms.

5. If Superstition kept back the progress of science in bygone days, Atheism under the name of Agnosticism is surely the drag put on in these our days. The marvellous juxtapositions of

well-shaped atoms pourtray miraculously the pre-design and the arranging of an Intelligent Power in Chemistry. Yes, but are not the Shapes of the Inorganic purely accidental, formed of necessity from the external conditions under which they take Shape? Are not crystals but enlarged geometric Shapes formed of necessity by the aggregating together of minute geometric molecular Shapes? On the whole, are not the various, accidental, surrounding pressures altogether the cause of the Shaping of the Inorganic Shapes? Truly, a vast number of Shapes are formed purely accidentally. Many such are found, for instance, in the realms of Geology and Geography. Yet, it is a question after all if on the whole the Shapes of such realms are really accidental. Even if they are, may they not then be permitted so to be for the sake of the romantic beauty shewn in their irregularity, and therefore, being so permitted, as they certainly are, they are not then strictly accidental. Let it be granted that the large, geometric crystal-Shapes are formed of necessity by minute geometric molecular-shapes, and these again by the particular nature or the atomic-Shapes, then what gave the particular nature to the atomic-Shapes? or, what makes them hold together or cohere in their particular Shapes? or, what makes the molecules or the crystals hold together or cohere in their Shapes? Is it not altogether evident design? Let it be even granted also that the various, accidental, surrounding pressures give the shapes, then what is the general cause of the surrounding pressure? Are not the surrounding pressures but that universal gravity, coherency, or holding together of substance by Will-pressure? If you say that it is just the general pressure of the general store of Motion in the universe, then that general store of Motion we say has originated, as it must, somewhere out of Will-action. And if you say that unconscious matter with Force or Motion is the thing eternal, still the fact remains that our spirits are conscious Substances capable of wielding force or motion by the action of their wills, and of moulding and shaping shapes of matter, then, wedged out conscious Substances come from but from the great mass of universal Spirit-Substance which is universal Matter, and that unmistakably is conscious.

So that, as for Shapes being shaped by surrounding pressures, and by the already formed Shapes of the ultimate particles which go together to make Shapes, it just comes to this: —What causes the surrounding pressures? And what has given the already formed ultimate particles their Shapes?

6. Then, as for the uniformity of the action in the Universal Pressure of Substance against Substance as shown in what is designated as the fixed laws of gravitation or cohesion, its very uniformity, which has been to many a stumbling-block, by making them imagine that it was a first cause in itself, its very uniformity or fixed mode of action shows the benignity and wisdom of the Great Will who so acts.

It shows His consideration for His creatures, for unless He acted uniformly so in such a manner as they could depend upon, they would be thrown into utter confusion, and would have no solid ground on which to rest. Unless men could depend upon the certain, so to speak, probability of the law of gravitation continuing in force in the manner in which it has continued, they would never rear their cities or build anything, for there would be no guarantee of their works standing. And yet, although of the mercy of God we have from and by Himself this "Recognised Law," still of the same mercy we have more: for in all our experiences in life we have at certain junctures His special interposition and interference for our good, which does not happen by mere coincidence of recognised law.

7. By the way a bit of the old song. Will-action or Will-Pressure or Will-Force is that which creates Motion. And that which holds something in a Shape is what? That which holds Substance in any particular Shape, what can it be but "Will-action-pressure-or-force?" What could else? And there is the Inorganic, and there

is the Organic they say. The inorganic is particularly the great mass of the spirit-substance of God; and the Organic is a portion thereof well built and prepared—a metropolis of mansions to receive the offspring of this One God.

8. Now, it is well to know as much of God as we can. And I am curious about His being, and I am delighted to find the All actually in all. Along the ages none ever doubted the existence of the sun, but many had strange ideas concerning it. And along the ages the eternal. power and godhead of the Great Being were clearly seen, being understood by the things made. But strange have been the ideas about Him. What is Truth? Truth is "Things as they are." Existence itself falls upon necessity. There is the basis. And what other means could the Great Power employ better than that of perpetually evincing evident Design in the Shapes of His creation to make known to other intelligent beings His own Intelligence? Would apparitions convince sceptics? No, they would frighten, or lead them to think there were many Gods. Any other method we can think of, if different from that employed, would be undignified, inconsistent and vain. Is it right on every occasion of a whim of doubt arising in our minds, to seek a special sign or miracle from the Almighty? Should not one sign be sufficient? We, of little faith!

9. Those complete Shapes, then, in which Substance holds itself are the manifestations of Intelligence: For that those complete Shapes in which Substance actually does choose to hold itself are not the manifestations of Intelligence is quite unthinkable.

10. N.B.—Those Complete Shapes: And not fragments. Let this hint suffice.

11. Before leaving let me name "Protoplasm." And let me give Roscoe's idea of it that it could not come together chemically, as it is not a chemical compound, but a compound of miraculous structures.

MOTION AND SHAPES.

TRUTH XXXI

MOTION AND SHAPES ARE ENTIRELY DEPENDENT UPON SUBSTANCE, SPACE AND TIME.

SELF-EVIDENCE OF TRUTH XXXI

Can you think of Motion and Shapes as independent or existing apart from Substance, Space and Time? No. Why, try to suppose either Motion or Shapes as independent or existing apart from Substance, Space and Time, and you will perceive that if there be Motion there must then be a Substance moving in Space and in Time, and if there be a Shape or Shapes there must then be a Substance making the Shape or Shapes in Space and in Time. So therefore, Motion and Shapes are entirely dependent on Substance, Space and Time: As it is unthinkable otherwise.

COMMENTS ON TRUTH XXXI

1. This truth is very plain and very self-evident. For, that Motion and Shapes could be without Substance, Space and Time is quite unthinkable.

2. But on the other hand, are Substance, Space and Time entirely independent of Motion and Shapes? Can Substance, Space and Time exist of themselves without Motion, and more especially without Shapes? Well, Time is not Motion and has no Motion though we sometimes speak of its speed; nor has Time any Shape or Shapes. Space is eternally immoveable in itself; and as for its Shape or Shapes, Shapes of parts of Space are merely imaginary, Space itself on the whole—unlimited Space

is not or has not a Shape. Substance, though in a state fluid to its infinitesimal depths, yet we can think of it remaining quiescent, motionless; ay, we can think of it even apart from Force, apart from Power of Holding together, that Pressure all round in together upon itself: why, is it not this Force that really makes the Shapes in Substance? Without this Force would Substance really be without Shape? Well, were Substance of endless extent throughout all Space, it could not be said then to have a Shape in its infinity; but, as it is, with vacuities within it, we cannot think of it without Shape of some sort, though that is perpetually altering; and further, were Substance nor Spirit, it would be found eternally without Motion and without Force and in monstrous irregularity instead of in the sublimely regular atomic Shapes, etc., in which we find it holding itself.

3. Motion and Shapes give grand scope of action for the great Spirit-substance existent in Space and Time. How sublime is the Sphere-Shape prominent throughout all the universe, nevertheless, the Sphere-Shape is easily departed from when it becomes expedient for the benefit of conscious being; this in itself shows Mind and Will. It may not be out of place here to note that interesting Geologic theory of "Wheel within Wheel". Taking the nebular hypothesis of the formation of the worlds then: when the external crust of the earth forming on the surface of the molten matter became of a certain thickness it would arch firm all round, and the internal, molten matter cooling and contracting would detach from it and form a globe within a globe, so to speak, with a spacious atmosphere between. This interior globe likewise forming a crust upon its surface, and the interior again still cooling and contracting, at length another interior globe would be formed. And so on in this process there might be formed a dozen globes or so nested within each other: the earth being eight thousand miles through, and giving two hundred miles as a sufficient thickness for each crust. Now, if anyone, thinking the earth was solid to the core, should have

wondered at the waste of Force shut up therein, and should have been apt to question Divine wisdom about it; let such an one consider this Geologic theory of "Wheel within Wheel." And who knows but that universal, solid Substance may be thus arranged, "Circle within Circle," in universal Space, and that we with all our visible, starry cosmos may be merely floating in one of the mighty atmospheres that lie Betwixt.

4. Are Shapes conscious things? Well, abstract Shapes, mere Abstractions are not in themselves conscious things. But is the Substance of each Shape conscious? Is this solid piece of timber conscious? Are these stones, and is this wall conscious?

Well, the Substance of each Shape is but a part of the great, universal, conscious, Spirit-mass. And when we touch any particular part or point thereof, the whole universal mass of Spirit-Substance must be conscious of being touched thereat.

Why, science proves at any rate that the slightest Motion effects to some degree the whole universe. Let us consider our own Spirits: they must have external surface though it be ever changing Shape. If a part is conscious the whole is conscious.

A portion or segment of the surface of any of our own souls is not in itself a separate conscious being, but would be so were it detached. And so the Substances of the various Shapes are not separate, conscious beings unless they be totally disconnected and detached from the universal mass. Our spirits are in contact with the universal mass, but " contact " is not "connexion." Spirit, having existence as a thing, it must have dimension And God, the Great Spirit, being the essential Substance of material things, is therefore actually "The All in All." And to point to the Shapes of things material and say that these then are God, is as much as to say that portions or segments of the surfaces of our own souls are ourselves.

TRUTH XXXII

MOTION AND SHAPES CONSTITUTE CREATED BEING OR EXISTENCE.

SELF-EVIDENCE OF TRUTH XXXII

Can you think what otherwise could constitute created being or existence but Motion and shapes? No. Why, try and suppose what within Space a creation by and from pre-existent Spirit-Substance could be, and you will perceive that such pre-existent Substance could only Move itself into new ways or into new systems of Shapes, and that as Motion is created by an act of will, and Shapes held in being by Force so created, Motion and Shapes then are verily a Creation. So therefore, Motion and Shapes constitute created being or existence: As it is unthinkable otherwise.

COMMENTS ON TRUTH XXXII

1. Compare this Truth XXXII with Truth XIX and see how well they couple together.

2. Motion and Shapes exist in Space but they do not occupy Space. Substance alone occupies Space.

3. We really cannot think what otherwise a creation could be but a Motion of pre-existent Substance into a new system of Shapes.

4: Behold! In the midst of the Divine, Eternal Essence arises the creation, and by the Divine Will it is upheld! At Will-Action Motion begins, and at the continuance of the Will-Action' the moving portions Press together and Shapes are formed. And the Shapes are swayed about in harmony according to the mind and by the will of The Great Spirit, the Eternal Essence. In very deed the Creation is upheld by the Will of God, and that literally, as says St. Paul, "He upholdeth all things by the Word of His Power."

5. Substance is in or within the Shapes, and Substance makes the Shapes, but Substance is not the Shapes. Now we have a clear conception of how the great Spirit, God, is All and in All.

6. Did God create the world out of nothing? Out of No-thing, No-thing comes. But what is a Thing? Here we perceive where the point is. The whole question of creation out of nothing lies in how we, define what a "Thing" is. No thing from no thing certainly if we define "thing" to be a something substantial or Substance. Then is the world not a something substantial or Substance? No, Substance makes and upholds the World, but the World is a mere Shape, and Shapes are not Substance, neither is Motion, and we easily can conceive of Motion an of Shapes being created in the true sense of the term. So Motion and Shapes constitute the Creation. If you like, conclude that Motion and Shapes are not "Things," but nevertheless you must admit them to be realities. The "That" which Moves, the "That" which underlies the Shape or Shapes is the Spirit-Substance of God who is the Uncreated. Could He have come out of nothing? He came never into being at all but was from everlasting to everlasting.

7. Some one will say that Motion and Shapes are neither Being nor Existence, that they necessitate a something Moving and a something being Shaped, and cannot exist of themselves as has been said, and are therefore merely modes of Being or Existence. Very well then, they Be or Exist as modes of that something which is alone to be considered as Being or Existence. But that something which alone is to be considered as Being or Existence cannot Be or Exist of itself but requires time and requires Space. So that Time and Space which could be or exist without anything seem to be still more self-existent. And why then call Substance alone Being or Existence? Time, Space, Substance, Motion and Shapes are the total of Being or Existence; and

Motion and Shapes are most essential realities thereof, and they constitute the creation.

8. Let us note here the difference betwixt impossibilities and inconceivabilities. The former should refer properly to the scope or action of Power or Motion; the latter to the utterly non-existent. Things impossible with men then may be possible with God. Things for which man is unable God may be able. Man cannot sway the stars or split atoms but he can conceive how God, being in and over all, may do so easily. Miracles are not inconceivabilities. How miracles are wrought is quite within the range of thinkability; only, man perceives how, though he be unable to accomplish them, God may accomplish them. But man plainly perceives that God cannot accomplish an inconceivability. Can God stay the current of Time? Can God go outside of Space? Can God annihilate the Substance of Himself? Can God make aught Move and yet not Move at one and the same instant? Can God make the mathematic or geometric truths involved in Shapes otherwise than they are? No.

Inconceivabilities are not things to be done at all. They are fallacies in speech, contradictions, direct contradictions if examined carefully. God, say some people, couldn't make a hill without a hollow. Of course not. Being cannot be and yet not be at one and the same time. There is no universe of things inconceivable.

Inconceivabilities are not things at all, they are nonextant. Being or existence is because it is, and God is the soul of Being or Existence which is from everlasting to everlasting. His great power of possibility lies in the physical realm of Motion and Shapes. The mathematic realm or realm of absolute truth is fixed and immovable.

9. That what otherwise a creation could be but a system of Motions and Shapes is quite unthinkable.

TIME, SPACE, SUBSTANCE, MOTION AND SHAPES.

TRUTH XXXIII

TIME, SPACE, SUBSTANCE, MOTION AND SHAPES ARE THE ENTIRE TOTAL OF ALL BEING OR EXISTENCE.

SELF-EVIDENCE OF TRUTH XXXIII.

Can you think of aught else besides Time, Space, Substance, Motion, Shapes? No. Why, try to suppose aught else besides Time, Space, Substance, Motion, Shapes, and you will perceive that you can only have as it were utter Non-being or Non-existence in the background, if perchance you can possibly conceive even that. So therefore, Time, Space, Substance, Motion and Shapes are the entire total of all Being or Existence: As it is unthinkable otherwise.

COMMENTS ON TRUTH XXXIII

1. Utter-Nothingness, shall it be brought in so as to make the Entire Total more complete? Utter-Nothingness as Utter-Nothingness in its fullest sense has no Being or Existence at all, for Space, pure Space everywhere excludes the possibility, ay even the very idea of it.

2. Time is but Time, Space but Space, Substance but Substance, Motion but Motion, Shapes but Shapes, in this sense, that they are but themselves, the only elementary or simple realities extant, all else being but combinations of them. Look at History, and Time comes out as a chief constituent with the other realities

inter-related; look at Mathematics, and Space comes out the same; look at Astronomy, Chemistry and Physiology, and Shapes come out the same; look at Physics, Light, Heat, Electricity, etc., and Motion comes out the same; look at the Universe, look at God, look at the Association of Sentient Things, and the Great Substance-Spirit comes out in its internal or conscious aspect, as well as in its external or material aspect, the same. A true idea of anything can only be had by analysing and realising such in the light of the Five Realities.

3. The Ancients had four, viz., Fire, Air, Earth and Water. But here are the foundational Five, —Time, Space, Substance, Motion, and Shapes

4. Time and Space on the one hand, Motion and Shapes on the other, and chief and central The Great Substance-Spirit of whom are all spirits: Here the entire total of all Existence or Being; Here the Absolute, the Complete.

5. Now, although these be the Entire Total, and although there be nought else existent outside or beyond these, as it is unthinkable there could be, nevertheless, Substance being Spirit, it has all the properties, qualities or attributes that common orthodoxy usually ascribes to Spirit. So that instead of Mind and Will being excluded from the total Five, they are more than included in the fact that Substance is conscious, is Spirit. Is not "hate" but a strong will to oppose and thwart, and is not "love" but a strong will to side with and aid? That inherent power of Will-Action which common orthodoxy usually ascribes to Spirit is here ascribed to Substance, and this hitherto undiscovered cause of coherency or holding together of Substance is a last discovered. That power which Spirit-Substance has of altering its shape at will is universally acknowledged: so that it is a power then that does inhere in a Substance. And what now will the old orthodoxists say about their inane, immaterial "Spirit"? There is actually no place found for it: and it is no where, and it never was, and

it never can be. It does not exist because it cannot. Boldly let me say to you who must have a God outside of Time and Space and separated apart altogether from Substance—let me say boldly to you that There is no such a God. Nor do I admit that there may be, for did I admit so I might then admit as well that two and two in some parts of the universe could be five and that any and every unthinkable thing could also exist. No, the God I believe in and adore and love is the God in whom I live, move and have my being, the God who environs me about. I am a conscious being, yes, but conscious of what? Principally of my environment. All my happiness is from thence, and my happiness overflows when I consider that the Substratum, Substance, or Essence of my Environment is actually the Substance of the Great, Conscious Spirit who loves, and has thus prepared Himself for, me. I must obey Him for I perceive that His laws fit in and square with the necessity of things. He is reasonable, and His will must prevail.

6. Time, Space, Substance, Motion, Shapes are, and Nought else is but what belongs thereto. These are the Primal Five—Five Realities. They are all-embracing. In them the whole of Being or Existence is seen as in a map. And that there is aught apart from, or beyond these is quite unthinkable. They include all and exclude Nothing. Time and Space: Substance; Motion and Shapes.

7. Substance has its two aspects —its internal aspect, and its external aspect. Its internal aspect is its consciousness, and the consequence of its Consciousness is the whole range of thought. Its external aspect is its solid, objective existence, and the consequence of its solid, objective existence is the whole material range. Out of its consciousness or internal aspect Substance Acts and Its Action appears as Force Or Motion in its external or material aspect.

8. There is, then, Within Time And Space A Substance Which Is In Motion And In Shapes.

9. To conclude then, Time and Space on the one hand, Motion and Shapes on the other, and chief and central, the Great Substance Spirit of whom are all Spirits. This the entire total of all existence or being, this the absolute. Substance universal is the Great, Uncreated One who is because He is, Time and Space are His abode, Motion and Shapes are His works. We look upon all spirits then as having come from this Great Universal Spirit. This Great Spirit is God; He is the Father of all spirits.

And is He not infinite? And what then can be taken from or added to the Infinite that can make the Infinite less or more. All human spirits of or from the Great Spirit, specks or particles of the Great Spirit, parts detached or portions disintegrated from the Great Spirit-but the Great Spirit still Infinite. All super-human spirits, angels, archangels, etc., whether in rebellion against Him or not, all of or from Him, parts or portions detached or disintegrated from Him, the Great Spirit-and He still infinite.

All supra-human spirits those in animal or plant organisms down to the infinitesimal animalcula, all specks or particles, parts or portions, detached or disintegrated or evolved of or from The Great Spirit—and the Great Spirit still Infinite. Yes.

What can lessen the Infinite? All spirits however of or from Him are nevertheless infinite in their own infinitesimality. They have all their rights and capabilities of Motion in their own spheres as they are all so many wills. And as it is evident that the action of each one tells upon and affects all, each one should see to it for his own good that his action be to the benefit of all. And yet considering them all as hanging upon the offences will come pivots of their "Wills", it is impossible but that as they are all free to take the wrong side as well as the right side, but no one need take the wrong side, therefore, "Woe to him through whom the offence comes."

10. It is astonishing to find that Locke had as clear an idea of the Substance of spirit as he had of the Substance of matter. He perceived the communication of Motion by thought as well as by impulse. He acknowledged the mystery of the coherency of matter or the mystery of the universal pressure. And yet he failed to clench the facts that Substance was conscious, was Spirit, and that by its will it cohered, or that its will-action originated the universal pressure.

TRUTH XXXIV

BEING OR EXISTENCE IS AS IT IS.

SELF-EVIDENCE OF TRUTH XXXIV

Can you think of Being or Existence as being otherwise than it is? No. Why, try to suppose Being or Existence as existing otherwise than it does exist, and you will plainly perceive that Being or Existence must be or exist as it actually does be or exist. So therefore, Being or Existence is as it is: as it is unthinkable otherwise.

COMMENTS ON TRUTH XXXIV

1. "As it is quite thinkable but unthinkable otherwise." — This has been our argument throughout all our study of Being or Existence. And taking all the Truths of Being or Existence together, we declare that not only now is it impossible that we can think otherwise about Being or Existence, but it is impossible that Being or Existence could be otherwise. Jehovah could not have it otherwise. Jehovah is not otherwise than he is.

2. "I think, therefore, I am." And since I am, there must be Space for me to be in, and there must be Time. And therefore, I am a conscious Thing, a Substance in Space and in Time. And

so Being or Existence actually is or exists, and a Something then must have been, and must be eternal — a Something Conscious: sure as the most certain sure. I myself a conscious being of one's self then is conscious only of what comes into contact with or affects its conscious self. Being or Existence constantly affects it, and so of Being or Existence it is constantly conscious.

Memory is not the conscious being of one's self, or it would never be out the consciousness. Memory must be markings, tracings or impressions chiefly upon the surfaces of that material environment with which the conscious substance of one's self frequently comes in contact. Memory of a sort too, but exceedingly transient, might possibly be markings, impressions, or tracings upon the active, conscious substance itself.

This conscious being of one's self, conscious of course of things which affect it, is conscious also of the differences betwixt things which affect it: and this consciousness of the differences betwixt things which affect it, is called "thought."

The more the number of different things which affect it, the more the "thought"; and the less the number, the less the "thought." If therefore, but one thing only affected the conscious being, the conscious being, although conscious of it, yet having nought where-with to compare a difference, would not have any "thought" concerning it. To be constantly conscious of but one thing is not "thought." And although conscious being be in itself a conscious substance, yet, if nothing affects it, it can have nothing even to be conscious of.

Supposing now this conscious being of one's self, this conscious entity, were carried away into pure, blank, empty space. And supposing it were left alone, with not a substance external to itself affecting it, and motionless there, what in that condition would it be conscious of? Would it have nought to be conscious of? And would it, therefore, remain forever motionless in that condition, unless something external to itself affected it? Well, if it had nought to be conscious of, it would remain for ever so, but it would have the difference betwixt itself and its empty environment, "Space," to be conscious of, and that "thought" would supply a motive for its voluntary action; and in its voluntary action it would become conscious of "Time" and although, in its voluntary action, it would be unconscious of any resisting, tangible environment as in such a condition as we have been supposing, there would be no resisting, tangible environment to be conscious of, yet, by moving some part or parts of itself against some other part or parts of itself, it would come to be conscious of the "Substance" of itself, and to be conscious of "Motion", and to be conscious of "Shapes"; thus to be conscious of all what Being or Existence is, from feeling the very nature of those primal Five realities.

3. This soul or spirit, this thing or entity, this conscious being of one's self is not in itself " thought " then. It is the that which thinks. Although it exists always a conscious thing, it may not always have the consciousness of certain things, for it may not always have certain things to be conscious of. And although its consciousness of things is not a motion, it is hard to think of it itself remaining long motionless, for its voluntary power of motion or action is so liable to be exercised over the objects of its consciousness.

As therefore we exist as conscious beings, conscious substances, we cannot but be conscious of the conditions under which we are placed. And thus we are conscious that Existence exists in the actual way in which it does exist, and that Existence does not exist otherwise than the actual way in which it exists. And the actual way in which it does exist is the actual state of things, the actual truth of the case; for it is the actual truth of the case, the actual state of the things themselves, the actual truth itself, which affects the conscious self. We then are conscious, existent entities, conscious of existence outside of ourselves, and therefore that we are but parts of the all of being or existence. And to think is simply to be conscious of the differences of things. This then is personal identity, the especial that of each of us which is conscious. The conditions under which that is placed is what it is conscious of.

So it itself and its environment are almost both of equal, essential importance. At present in Him we live, move and have our being, but let it be our eternal ambition to have Him always as our environment, with His Will and ours in unison. At present He upholds the earth for us upon which we stand, and He upholds those organisms of ours by which we come into harmony with His creation and live. So to reciprocate, let it be our constant and eternal effort to find out always what His will with us is and to obey it. And we then shall always have an environment of Substance, and that substance will be the Substance of the Great Spirit, God. And our wills shall be in unison.

4. That thing then which thinks, that piece of conscious being which is the conscious self—it exists. It has the power of voluntary action, for it acts. So we exist: and the realities of Being or Existence — they exist. Time, Space, Substance, Motion, Shapes, exist. In the mode in which things actually are, things exist.

And so agnosticism concerning such realities will not serve us in our action with them, for we have to deal with them as they are, or if we refuse to deal with them they will, nevertheless, necessarily deal with us.

We together with them are involved in the necessity of things. Let us awake to know our power and theirs. Agnosticism satisfieth not. We act in daily life upon the average without agnosticism. We act as that we fully know what we are doing, as that we fully know the certainties of the realities with which, and conditions under which, we are acting. To act otherwise is foolish acting. To act habitually under agnosticism shows a dull stupidity, and is decidedly suicidal.

5. In Being or Existence then, whatever is, is, and is not otherwise than it is, for its being otherwise than it is will be unthinkable. And whatever is presented to the conscious thing is also as it is, and the conscious thing cannot be conscious of it otherwise than it is, but must think about it and know it to be as it is and not otherwise.

Whatever we cannot think, or whatever is unthinkable when given us to think, has then no existence or being whatever. Or rather, whatever we cannot conceive, or whatever is inconceivable when given us to conceive, has no being or existence whatever. For instance, can two and two ever be more or less than four? Can an eagle be flying eastward and westward at one and the same time? Can a part ever be greater than the whole? Can the past be as that it never had been?

Can a thing be and yet not be at one and the same time? No. Not even to God can these and such as these be. They are quite unthinkable, quite inconceivable, because they actually are not and cannot even be: as only what actually is or what can possibly be will affect the conscious thing and so be thought of. Such then have no existence at all as they are quite unthinkable, quite inconceivable. If you like, the truth concerning them can be proved by experiment in this way, that either of them cannot be done, so to speak, if attempted.

The Truths concerning Being or Existence as set forth in the foregoing pages are based upon this then that Things are quite thinkable taking them as they are, but taking them otherwise than they are they are quite unthinkable and can have therefore no existence so.

This is the sum of the Truths set forth: This, that the five realities —Time, Space, Substance, Motion and Shapes, are the entire total of all Being or Existence; that Time, Space and Substance could never have begun to be and can never cease to be, but that Motion and Shapes may begin to be and may cease to be; that

Substance is the that that is conscious; that at will Substance moves itself and thus creates Motion; and that at will Substance holds itself together in multitudinous, various Shapes; and that those multitudinous, various Shapes constitute the creation. This, then, is the Truth about Being or Existence: and the argument is, that Being or Existence is unthinkable otherwise. In the foregoing pages we have used simple words. Complex words give opportunity for mental jugglery: and there are some dishonest thinkers who are not slow to take undue advantage of fallacies arising from complex words.

And so then, we accept the Truths upon the basis of thinkability about them; if you reject them because you think that thinkability about them is not umpire, then, just by so thinking, and by rejecting them just upon the strength of so thinking, you verily acknowledge that thinkability is umpire.

6. Being or Existence thus actually is or exists, and whatever is unthinkable has no being or existence whatever: for it is altogether unthinkable that Being or Existence is or does exist otherwise than it actually is or does exist.

7. After all, What is it all for? Is it for the sake of Truth? Yes. But, what actually is Truth? Truth is "Things as They Are." To know Things as they Are is to have the Light of Truth, and to have the Light of Truth is to see clearly How to Act. But To Know is one thing, and To Act is another.

8. To know God, The Great Spirit, Our Environment, The All and In All, and to correspond, to commune, our spirits with His Spirit and His Spirit with our spirits; And to be conscious each of each other in Love: This is the "Highest Good." To know that we ourselves are all so the speak so many "wills," and that God Himself is the Great "Will." And to have the common sense from the circumstances of the case to see that the lesser "wills" ought to give way to the higher wisdom of the Great "Will." And here is the reward for good behaviour: "He that doeth the Will of God

shall abide forever." Not every one that saith unto me, "Lord, Lord," shall enter into the kingdom of heaven, but he that doeth the will of my father which is in heaven.

9. The Government of the universe is found to be based upon Power. Each spirit has its own action at will, but what spirit can stand before the Action of the Almighty Spirit when He Wills to avenge. Fear Him who is able to destroy both soul and body in hell. Our God is a consuming fire. Our individuality of both body and spirit He can destroy though He can annihilate not the essence of spirit for how could He annihilate essence of Himself.

10. Then this is what it is all for. Having found out that God is All and in All, to accept Him then as Our All and in All. If we do not this our search after Truth even though we find it, is in vain. Let us but have a commonsense attitude before the Necessity of Things. And this is a commonsense attitude when our spirits in sincerity say "Thy Will be Done." Let us keep ourselves in the Love of God and the main end is not missed. But let this be added as a final idea, that the Will of God must be done if we would abide for ever. So that this then is the parting word, "He that doeth the will of God abideth for ever."

MORE TITLES AVAILABLE BY FAUUN

The Kybalion — Three Initiates

The Science of Getting Rich — Wallace D Wattles

Think and Grow Rich — Napoleon Hill

Dreams and Dream Stories — Anna Kingsford

Proofs of the Spirit World (On Ne Meurt Pas) — Léon Chevreuil

The Richest Man in Babylon — George S Clason

Moonchild — Aleister Crowley

The Seawitch Tarot — Willow Whiteraven

The Deepest Secret — Bel Bare

Our titles are unfurling into a collection of classics, gothic, erotic, occult, spirituality, poetry, fables, and original literature.
We are proud to improve access to titles that have previously not been redesigned since their original publication, making the reader experience more enjoyable.

Fauun was founded in Australia by designer, artist, author, and occultist Bel Bare. Fusing her love of books, passion for the mysterious, and insatiable curiosity, lifetimes of studying literature and the supernatural have manifested into Fauun.

WWW.FAUUN.COM

www.ingramcontent.com/pod-product-compliance
Lightning Source LLC
Chambersburg PA
CBHW051527220426
43209CB00107B/1988/J